Comics Startup 101:

Key Legal and Business Issues for Comic

Book Creators

By Dirk Vanover

Some of the material in this book first appeared on ComicsLawyer.com

Cover art by Douglas Paszkiewicz.

© 2017 Dirk Vanover. Except for educational uses, no portion of this book may be used or reproduced without the author's written permission.

Contents

Disclaimer 5
Introduction 6
I.   The Beginning – A Clearance Search 7
II.   Diving In – Choosing a Business Entity 9
   a.   Sole Proprietorship 9
   b.   Limited Liability Company 10
      i.)   Single-member LLC 10
      ii.)   Multi-member LLC 11
   c.   Corporations 11
      i.)   S Corporation 11
III. Contracts 12
   a.   Negotiating power 12
   b.   Your own contracts 12
   c.   Contracts from other parties 14
IV. Intellectual Property 16
   a.   Overview 16
   b.   Protecting Your Intellectual Property 18
      i.)   Copyright 18
      ii.)   Work Made for Hire 19
      iii.) Trademark 23
      iv.) Domains 23
      v.)   Using the DMCA Takedown Notice 24
   c.   The Infringement of Others' Intellectual Property ... 27
   d.   Fan Art, Fair Use, and the First Amendment 31
V.   Who Owns Superman? 37

VI.	Putting it Together – A Contract Walk Through	44
VII.	Conclusion	51
About the Author		52
Appendix A		53
Endnotes		59

Disclaimer

This book is not meant to be an in-depth guide, nor is it meant to be complete legal advice. Any information provided in this book is general in nature and should not be relied upon as legal advice. Meaningful legal advice cannot be given without a full understanding of all relevant facts relating to an individual's situation. As such, you should consult with an attorney for specific legal advice that you might need.

Introduction

Congratulations! If you are reading this, then you have an idea for a comic book and want to create it yourself. This book grew out of a panel I presented with comic book creators at various comic book conventions in the Midwest and from the posts on my ComicsLawyer.com blog. Hopefully, you will find what follows to be a helpful guide when proceeding down the path of creating your own comic book, or if you do not end up making a comic, I hope you'll find this information helpful for any other business endeavor you start.

This leads me to one of the best pieces of advice that I can give you: develop a great support team you can trust to help you on your journey. I recommend this to any small business owner, which you are about to become. Your support team should consist of at least these three people: a mentor or advisor, an accountant, and an attorney. It is helpful to have a mentor or advisor who has done what you want to do, can act as a guide on your journey, and can act as a resource to bounce ideas off of. Unless you are extremely knowledgeable about tax law, I also recommend an accountant. A great accountant should be able to provide you with the advice you'll need to properly run your business and not run afoul of the IRS. An attorney, much like the mentor and accountant, can be an invaluable resource. The proper attorney can help guide you and your business so as to prevent legal troubles before they can derail your career. Even though the cost of utilizing these professionals might seem daunting, it is better to pay that expense upfront to avoid even more expensive trouble later. Additionally, there are resources out there to service struggling artists by putting them in contact with professionals who can assist them with free or low-cost services, such as the Volunteer Lawyers for the Arts, Volunteer Lawyers and Accountants for the Arts, and the Lawyers for the Creative Arts. If cost is a concern for you, seek out a similar organization. Additionally, if you want to learn more about the sources I use and quote in this book, look up the corresponding endnotes. Most of the resources I used are available for free.

Now, let's take your idea for a comic book and start at the beginning.

I.   The Beginning – A Clearance Search

You have an idea for a comic book. What's next? One of the first things you should do is conduct a clearance search. By conducting a clearance search you will make sure that no one else is making a comic with the same title, a similarly named character, or a character that is too closely related by way of powers, origins, background, etc. Doing this simple step early could save you a lot of trouble and money later on. It also allows you to distinguish your creation from other characters and, if used properly, gives you the ability to create something unique.

For an example of why doing a clearance search is a good idea, let's look to Fawcett Publications and their Captain Marvel character. Captain Marvel was a character originally created by Fawcett Publications[1] shortly after Superman was created. Many of you now know the character as Shazam.[2] National Comics Publications, previously known as Detective Comics, Inc., believed that Captain Marvel infringed on their Superman copyrights.[3] After a twelve year legal battle, the Second Circuit Appeals Court found that National Comics had valid copyrights in Superman[4] and that Fawcett's Captain Marvel infringed upon them.[5] While there was evidence presented at trial that Fawcett intentionally copied elements of Superman,[6] I believe this case would be decided differently today. These characters share some similar traits, but their origin stories differ significantly.[7] In the end, Fawcett agreed to settle and ceased printing Captain Marvel comics.[8] Eventually, DC Comics acquired the rights to Captain Marvel and started using the character in its own universe.[9] Further muddying the waters, during the time Fawcett ceased publishing Captain Marvel, Marvel Comics acquired the trademark rights to Captain Marvel as a publication name.[10] Since DC couldn't use Captain Marvel as a comic book title, they used *Shazam!* as the title instead. Even though a clearance search might not have saved Captain Marvel in this particular case, it shows the value of conducting a clearance search – if your character is too close in resemblance to another, you might be sued for infringement and lose the ability to exploit your creation.

To conduct a comprehensive, in-depth clearance search will cost you a few hundred dollars upwards to a few thousand. There are services out there that will conduct searches of registered trademarks, domains, business entities, general internet searches, and more for you. Most of these will uncover possible trademark conflicts. It is a bit harder to do a copyright search. However, if a copyrighted work is commercially exploited, you should be able to discover it by using similar methods. While it is highly recommended that you conduct a comprehensive clearance search utilizing an attorney or a company specializing in doing

such searches, if you want to conduct an initial search on your own to gauge potential risk, I would recommend the following steps:
1) searching the United States Patent and Trademark Office ("USPTO") trademark search database for your character's name or book's title,
2) searching the U.S. Copyright Office database for your character's name or book's title,
3) conduct a WHOIS domain registry search for domain names using your character's name or book's title, and
4) run a few internet searches for your character's name, book's title, and a description of your character, plot, powers, etc.

These searches are not guaranteed to uncover every potential risk, but they should give you an idea of whether something else is out there. If you are comfortable with what you've uncovered, then you may proceed at your own risk. Otherwise, if you are uncomfortable with what you've found, you may want to consult with an attorney.

II. Diving In – Choosing a Business Entity

You've conducted a clearance search and have decided to move forward with creating your comic. The next thing to consider is whether to form a corporation. As I mentioned before, this is a good time to discuss your goals with an attorney and accountant. They can help guide you in the process.

You do not have to form a corporation in order to create your comic. Many people are self-employed without doing so. However, the benefit of forming a corporation is that you limit your personal liability for your business.[11] Depending on your circumstances and the business you are forming, there can also be some tax benefits.[12] In this section, I'm going to primarily discuss the formation of a limited liability corporation. It is one of the most popular corporate entities for small businesses, and it is the easiest to form. Every state allows for the creation of LLCs. However, the laws and regulations governing an LLC vary by state.[13] You will have to choose the proper state for the creation of your LLC. Most likely, you will choose to form the LLC in the state where you reside or will conduct most of your business. However, some people choose to register in other states, such as Delaware, that cater more toward corporate entities. Cost, taxation, and personal residence and business location will be the main factors to consider in determining whether to form a corporation in your home state.

In determining whether or not to form a corporation, you will need to consider your risks, your ability to grow, and your ability to follow corporate formalities. If you are still uncertain about the longevity of your career as a comic creator, you may not want to form a corporation. If you do not believe there is much personal risk to you in creating this comic, then you may not want to form a corporation. If you are not very good at observing and following certain, specific procedural rules, then you may not want to form a corporation. If you form a corporation and fail to follow corporate formalities and certain procedures as required by law, or fail to operate the corporation as a separate entity, then you might lose the benefit of the limited liability the formation of the company provided. All of these factors should be considered when you are contemplating forming a corporation to conduct your business.

a. **Sole Proprietorship**

As I stated above, there is no requirement that you form a corporation in order to make your comic. There are many people out there who do not form a corporation to conduct business, including many comic book artists and writers. If you don't want to deal with the hassle and formalities of forming and running a corporation, you don't have to. You may conduct your business yourself. However, you will be responsible for all of your business' debt, liabilities, and losses. The main reason to form a business entity such as an LLC is to limit your personal liability for the expenses of the business.

b. Limited Liability Company

In order to create an LLC, you must file articles of organization with the proper state entity (Secretary of State, Department of Financial Institutions, etc.).[14] Depending on the state and the structure of your LLC, you may also have to draft and adopt an operating agreement to set forth the responsibilities of the members, liabilities, voting procedures, dissolution procedures, and many more issues.[15] You will also have to determine how your LLC will be taxed. Many LLCs are treated as separate tax entities, and instead of the LLC being taxed, the profits distributed to members are taxed on their personal income tax returns.[16] Different types of LLCs have different default tax classifications.[17] By consulting with an attorney and accountant, you can determine what LLC and tax classifications are the most appropriate for your business. As stated before, these rules can vary from state to state. One thing to keep in mind is the point of forming a corporation, other than for tax purposes, is to limit your liability. When you begin working with some companies, they may ask you to sign a personal guarantee in order to do business with them. Be careful signing such guarantees. If you sign a personal guarantee, then you will be personally responsible for any debts or liabilities your company incurs under that agreement.

i.) Single-member LLC

In many states, you may form a single-member LLC.[18] If you are going to be the only individual owning and running the company, then this might be your LLC of choice. A single-member LLC provides you with many of the same legal protections as a multi-member LLC. However, the primary difference between the two is how the IRS treats a single-member LLC. Unless you specifically opt out of it, the IRS will treat a single-member LLC as a disregarded entity for tax purposes.[19] This means that you will not have to file a separate tax return for your LLC. You will file the earnings and losses of your LLC along with your personal tax return. However, if you form a single-member LLC, I recommend keeping great records and taking all the necessary steps to maintain it as a separate entity from yourself. This is the best way to make sure you do not lose limited liability protection.

ii.) Multi-member LLC

A multi-member LLC is appropriate if your business will involve more than one person as an owner (member). The requirements are the same as for the single-member LLC. You must file the paperwork with the proper agency in your state. However, it is more important to draft and adopt an operating agreement when you are in a multi-member LLC. The operating agreement will govern how the LLC runs, and it will spell out how the owners of the LLC will interact with each other, get paid, and otherwise manage the affairs of the company. This means you need to address in writing the responsibilities of the members, liabilities, voting procedures, dissolution procedures, and many more issues.

c. Corporations

Even though I said I'd mostly focus on LLCs, I felt I needed to at least touch on corporations. Generally speaking, there are not many instances where a corporation would be the proper entity of choice for an independent comic book creator. Corporations are complex legal entities that require a significant amount of time and money to start and operate.[20] If you are just starting out making comics, then I would recommend an LLC or sole proprietorship. If your career is advancing and growing, you are diversifying your businesses, or seeking investors, then it could make sense to try and form a corporation. If you think a corporation might be right for you, please consult with your accountant and attorney.

i.) S Corporation

The S Corporation deserves a short mention based on possible tax benefits it confers.[21] The primary benefit of an S Corporation is that it avoids possible double taxation on a corporation (corporate income tax and shareholder tax).[22] However, there are specific requirements a corporation must meet before it can qualify as an S Corporation, such as being limited to only 100 shareholders and shareholders cannot be nonresident aliens.[23] Additionally, it is possible for an LLC to be taxed as an S Corporation, which could provide some tax savings.[24] In order to determine if an S Corporation or an LLC taxed as an S Corporation might be the right business entity for you, it is recommended you speak with your attorney and accountant, as the laws governing the taxation of these entities can vary from state to state.[25]

III. Contracts

I cannot stress enough how important contracts are to businesses. It is important that you have your own contracts in place for services you provide and the people you hire. It is also important that you pay attention to the contracts you sign with third parties. If you sign an agreement, then you are bound to all of the provisions contained in the contract.

a. Negotiating power

When you are presented with a contract, remember that it is a negotiation. If someone presents you with a contract to sign, read it. If you don't have questions about anything in the contract and have no objections to what is being stated in the contract, then you can sign it. If there are things you don't understand, ask for clarifications. If there is language in the agreement you are uncomfortable with, ask for changes. In most instances, the worst thing they will do is say no.

While negotiating contracts, do keep in mind which party has the negotiating power. Do you desperately want to work with them? Then they may have the negotiating power to dictate terms. Do they desperately want to work with you? Then you may have the negotiating power to change terms you dislike. Are there other options for you if the other party isn't willing to work with you? Then you have some leverage. Keep all of these in mind as you are negotiating your contracts, and remember, with great negotiating power comes great responsibility – use it wisely and don't abuse it.

b. Your own contracts

If you will be hiring others to work on your comic, you should have them sign a contract. The basics that should be in the agreement: how much you will pay them, what they will do for you, and when they will do it. It is also best to clearly spell out who owns the intellectual property, artwork, etc. Failing to do so could lead to major problems down the road.

For an example, look no further than the Angela saga involving Todd McFarlane and Neil Gaiman. In 1992, McFarlane asked Gaiman to write a story for his *Spawn* comic book series.[26] Gaiman and McFarlane did not have a written agreement outlining copyright ownership, "nor, for that matter, of how Gaiman would be compensated for his work, beyond McFarlane's assuring Gaiman that he would treat him "better than the big guys" did."[27] The story in question, *Spawn* No. 9, was a huge success[28] and introduced three new characters: Angela, Medieval Spawn, and Cogliostro.[29] Angela was very popular with the readers of the *Spawn* series, and McFarlane and Gaiman agreed to use her in her own miniseries.[30] Gaiman received periodic royalty payments from McFarlane, but eventually sought to have their oral agreement put into writing.[31] After some negotiation, they reached a tentative agreement where Gaiman would receive some royalty payments and the rights to another character McFarlane believed he owned in exchange for Gaiman's rights to Medieval Spawn and Cogliostro.[32] After a few years had passed, McFarlane sent a letter stating that all previous agreements were rescinded, and the only deal available was for Gaiman to give up any rights to Angela in exchange for McFarlane's rights in another character.[33] Gaiman claimed he was a co-owner of the characters in question and sued.[34] The Seventh Circuit Court of Appeals found that both owned an interest in the character,[35] and McFarlane conceded that Gaiman was a co-owner of Angela.[36] After a decade of litigation, the two sides settled,[37] with Gaiman ultimately transferring his rights to the character to Marvel Comics.[38] Had McFarlane and Gaiman entered into an agreement spelling out agreed upon compensation and ownership rights at the beginning of their relationship, a lengthy legal battle could have been avoided and Angela might still be in the *Spawn* universe.

Another example of how failing to clearly spell out each party's roles beforehand can come back to bite you arises from *The Walking Dead*. Robert Kirkman was the author and creator of the *The Walking Dead* comic book series, and his longtime friend Tony Moore was the original artist.[39] In 2012, Tony Moore, who had left the series after a few issues, sued Kirkman for royalties and a declaration that he was a co-creator of *The Walking Dead*.[40] Moore claimed that he was duped out of his rights in 2005 when he assigned any interest he might have in *The Walking Dead* to Kirkman and his company so that a television show could be produced.[41] In exchange he was promised royalties, which he claimed were not received.[42] Eventually, the parties settled before trial, and the details have remained confidential.[43]

This is mostly speculation on my part, but this mess could have been avoided if agreements were in place before Kirkman and Moore started making *The Walking Dead*. If they had signed an agreement stating that Kirkman owned all of the intellectual property rights to the comic, and Moore was just the artist, then Moore's claim that he was a co-creator would not have gone far. Based on the fact that Kirkman and his company asked Moore to assign rights in exchange for royalty payments years after the series began, it appears likely there was no contract between them. Eventually, Kirkman's team realized Moore had a possible claim to being a co-creator of the series, and they asked him to assign his rights to the series in an attempt to try and clean up the copyright rights to *The Walking Dead*.

Both of the previously mentioned disputes could have been avoided had the parties entered into an agreement at the beginning of their relationships clearing spelling out each person's duties, responsibilities, and rights. We will discuss this type of contract more in-depth in the Work Made for Hire section later in this book.

c. **Contracts from other parties**

When dealing with contracts you have received from other parties, keep in mind what we talked about in the sections on negotiating power and your own contracts. Key questions to ask yourself when you are reviewing a contract include:
- How much will it cost?
- What will I be doing for them?
- What will they be doing for me?
- What rights am I giving away?
- What rights am I getting?
- Who owns the intellectual property rights?
- Who is assuming the most risk under this agreement?
- Who is responsible if problems arise under the agreement?
- How long is the agreement?
- When does it end?
- Does this agreement automatically renew?
- Is it exclusive?
- Is there a right of first refusal?
- If I'm unhappy, how can I terminate this agreement?
- How can they terminate this agreement on me?
- When and where can I be sued?

These are some of the primary questions you should be asking, and the answers should be reflected in the agreement you are reading. You should also make sure that you understand every section, paragraph, and sentence of the agreement. You do not want to unknowingly give away your rights to your creation or give them an unlimited license to your work. One final tip, if an agreement seems too short, make sure they are not incorporating outside documents into the agreement. I have seen too many people read a one-page contract and fail to follow up with any other document mentioned in it or a hyperlink leading to additional terms and conditions buried in the agreement. Failing to do so could lead you to unwittingly agreeing to unfavorable contract terms.

For an example of making sure you understand everything in your contract and the possible ramifications, let us look at Alan Moore. He gave us, with Dave Gibbons, one of the most popular and revered graphic novels of all time: *Watchmen*. Since creating *Watchmen*, *V for Vendetta*, and many other notable titles for DC Comics and its imprints, Moore has had a falling out with the company. There are a host of issues Moore had during his tenure working with DC Comics that he was unhappy about, but one topic seems to keep coming up: the language in his contract that would return to him the rights to his creations when the comics went out of print.[44] This is a great example of making sure you understand the language in your contract and how it might apply. Moore is upset because this language allowing him to regain the rights to his creations was written into the contract, but the comics have proved so popular they have never gone out of print. While the language is in the contract, it has become meaningless. So long as DC continues to print *Watchmen* and *V: For Vendetta*, Moore will not see the rights to these creations returned to him. While it is easy to understand why he is upset by this situation, it sounds as if it was clearly spelled out in the agreements he signed. As stated previously, it is important to understand all of the language in the contracts you are agreeing to as well as the ramifications of that language.

IV. Intellectual Property

a. Overview

As a creator, you should be aware of the laws relating to intellectual property. Generally speaking, there are four areas of intellectual property law – patent, copyright, trademark, and trade secrets. A fifth area of law, right of publicity, is sometimes lumped in with intellectual property rights even though it arises from a person's right to privacy. In all likelihood, you will not have to worry about patents or trade secrets as you create your comic, and we will not discuss them here. Copyright, trademark, and right of publicity law will be important to you.

Copyright protection is granted by federal law.[45] It protects "original works of authorship fixed in any tangible medium of expression."[46] Included works of authorship are "(1) literary works; (2) musical works, including any accompanying words; (3) dramatic works, including any accompanying music; (4) pantomimes and choreographic works; (5) pictorial, graphic, and sculptural works; (6) motion pictures and other audiovisual works; (7) sound recordings; and (8) architectural works."[47] The Copyright Act grants exclusive rights to the creator of the work for the life of the creator plus 70 years,[48] or 95 years from the date of first publication or 120 years from the date of creation, whichever is shorter, for works made for hire, anonymous and pseudonymous works.[49] These exclusive rights include the right: "(1) to reproduce the copyrighted work in copies or phonorecords; (2) to prepare derivative works based upon the copyrighted work; (3) to distribute copies or phonorecords of the copyrighted work to the public by sale or other transfer of ownership, or by rental, lease, or lending; (4) in the case of literary, musical, dramatic, and choreographic works, pantomimes, and motion pictures and other audiovisual works, to perform the copyrighted work publicly; (5) in the case of literary, musical, dramatic, and choreographic works, pantomimes, and pictorial, graphic, or sculptural works, including the individual images of a motion picture or other audiovisual work, to display the copyrighted work publicly; and (6) in the case of sound recordings, to perform the copyrighted work publicly by means of a digital audio transmission."[50]

Technically, you do not need to register your copyright.[51] However, in order to enjoy the full benefits of copyright protection, you must register your copyrighted work with the U.S. Copyright Office within three months of publication of the work.[52] Some of the benefits of registration include 1) a public record of your copyright claim, 2) statutory damages and attorney's fees in an infringement lawsuit (if registration is filed within three months of publication), 3) and the ability to prevent the importation of infringing copies of your work.[53] A copyright registration may be filed with the Copyright Office at any time during the term of copyright protection, but there are certain benefits to registering early within the copyright term as we discussed above.[54]

Trademarks are used as source indicators for goods and services (also known as service marks).[55] Trademark rights can be protected as long as your trademark is in use, and, if the trademark is registered with the United States Patent and Trademark Office, you have filed all the required documents showing continued use of the trademark.[56] Trademark rights arise from use in commerce.[57] Generally speaking, the first person or company to use a trademark for their goods or services has acquired some rights to prevent others from doing so, even if the trademark is not registered with the USPTO.[58] However, in order to have the broadest protection available, a trademark should be registered with the USPTO. The benefits of registering a trademark with the USPTO include "[p]ublic notice of your claim of ownership of the mark; [a] legal presumption of your ownership of the mark and your exclusive right to use the mark nationwide on or in connection with the goods/services listed in the registration; [t]he ability to bring an action concerning the mark in federal court; [t]he use of the U.S. registration as a basis to obtain registration in foreign countries; [t]he ability to record the U.S. registration with the U.S. Customs and Border Protection (CBP) Service to prevent importation of infringing foreign goods; [t]he right to use the federal registration symbol ®; and [l]isting in the [USPTO]'s online databases."[59] It is important to note, however, that in order for a trademark to be registered with the federal government, it must be used in interstate commerce.[60]

The title of a book, play, or other creative work cannot be trademarked unless it is part of a series of creative works.[61] The reason for this comes from copyright law.[62] A trademark can last forever.[63] A copyrighted work must eventually fall into the public domain where anyone can use it or reproduce it without compensation to the original copyright holder. As such, one must be able to call the work "by the only name it has and the title cannot be withheld on any theory of trademark right...."[64] Since comic books are usually part of a series, they are entitled to receive trademark protection. However, a one-shot graphic novel would not be entitled to trademark protection.

It is possible for an image or logo to be eligible for both trademark and copyright protection.[65] For example, Superman's S shield arose as a copyrightable image/design, but it has also become an indicator of goods and services for DC Comics and a registered trademark for belt buckles,[66] toys,[67] sporting goods,[68] electronic games,[69] motion pictures,[70] comic magazines,[71] and many other types of goods. So, it is protected by both copyright and trademark law.

The right of publicity is the final area of law you will need to be aware of as a creator. Even though the right of publicity might not technically be an intellectual property right, it is nonetheless lumped in with these for good reason. Originally, the right of publicity arose out of a person's right to privacy.[72] However, as the law developed over time, it was accepted that in addition to a right to privacy, a person also has a right to control how their likeness is exploited for financial gain.[73] The right of publicity allows someone, typically a celebrity, to control how their image or likeness is exploited for commercial purposes.[74] The right of publicity has been adopted in some form in over half of the states.[75] The right differs from state to state and can apply to "sound-alikes; look-alikes; use of the celebrity's nickname in a fictional work; use of address; statues; and the use of a robot that barely resembles the celebrity but evokes her image."[76] Generally speaking from my own experience, the right of publicity is a very broad legal doctrine that can pose serious problems for creators trying to evoke the likeness of a living person or celebrity. If you do not have permission to use a living person's or celebrity's likeness in your creation, then you should proceed carefully.

b. Protecting Your Intellectual Property

In addition to understanding the basics of intellectual property laws, it is also important to understand how to protect your intellectual property rights. The key ways to protect your intellectual property rights are to register them, use contracts to preserve and protect your rights, and enforce your rights against anyone who might be infringing on your intellectual property.

i.) Copyright

As mentioned previously, copyright protects any "original works of authorship fixed in any tangible medium of expression."[77] The comic book that you are creating, when finished and offered for sale, is a copyrighted work entitled to protection under U.S. copyright law.

An important decision will need to be made about if or when you want to apply for copyright registration with the U.S. Copyright Office. You may register a copyright at any time.[78] However, you must register it within three months of its first publication in order to be granted full copyright protection, including statutory damages in the event of infringement litigation.[79] You also must register your copyright before you file a copyright infringement lawsuit.[80] If you do not register your work within three months of publication or before an infringement has occurred, then you are only entitled to seek actual damages and profits in a copyright infringement lawsuit.[81] The difference between being able to obtain statutory damages and recovering actual damages and profits can be substantial. When able, most copyright owners choose to seek statutory damages in a copyright infringement lawsuit because the damages awarded under the statute can be higher, ranging from as little as $200 up to $150,000 for each infringement depending on the circumstances of the case, and the copyright owner is not required to prove actual damages or profits in court.[82]

As of the writing of this book, the cost to register a copyright can vary from as little as $35 to as much as $85 or more, depending on the work you are seeking to register and the method you choose to register, i.e., electronic versus paper registration. You can check with the Copyright Office for the current fees. If you can afford to register your work with the Copyright Office, it is best to do so as soon as the work is published.

ii.)   Work Made for Hire

While it is important to understand the importance of registering your copyrighted work with the Copyright Office and requirements to do so, it is also necessary to understand how to protect your copyrighted work contractually. As we discussed in the section on using contracts and the McFarlane and Gaiman case, it is important to use contracts if you hire someone else to work on your creation. By using a contract, you will protect your intellectual property rights by entering into a work made for hire agreement with any freelancer you hire to work on your book. The work made for hire agreement should prevent her from acquiring a copyright interest in her contributions to your work.

What are we talking about when we talk about a work made for hire, also known as a work for hire? Basically, we are talking about work made by an employee for an employer, or a written agreement to create work specifically made by one party for a commissioning party that falls into one of the categories established in the 1976 Copyright Act. Under the work made for hire doctrine, the employer or the commissioning party are considered the authors of the work.

The 1976 Copyright Act defines a work made for hire as "a work prepared by an employee within the scope of his or her employment; or (2) a work specially ordered or commissioned for use [1] as a contribution to a collective work, [2]as a part of a motion picture or other audiovisual work, [3]as a translation, [4]as a supplementary work, [5]as a compilation, [6]as an instructional text, [7]as a test, [8]as answer material for a test, [9]or as an atlas, if the parties expressly agree in a written instrument signed by them that the work shall be considered a work made for hire. For the purpose of the foregoing sentence, a "supplementary work" is a work prepared for publication as a secondary adjunct to a work by another author for the purpose of introducing, concluding, illustrating, explaining, revising, commenting upon, or assisting in the use of the other work, such as forewords, afterwords, pictorial illustrations, maps, charts, tables, editorial notes, musical arrangements, answer material for tests, bibliographies, appendixes, and indexes, and an "instructional text" is a literary, pictorial, or graphic work prepared for publication and with the purpose of use in systematic instructional activities."[83] (Numerical brackets added for emphasis.) Later in the Act, it further adds that "the employer or other person for whom the work was prepared is considered the author for purposes of this title, and, unless the parties have expressly agreed otherwise in a written instrument signed by them, owns all of the rights comprised in the copyright."[84]

Under the Act, there are two ways a copyright eligible work you create might belong to another: (1) if you are an employee, and it relates to and was made during your employment, or (2) if you entered into a work made for hire agreement, and it falls into one of the nine categories listed in the previous paragraph.

If you are a creator, you need to be aware of the work made for hire doctrine and how it impacts you. First, if you are working as an employee for an employer, or in a relationship that can be categorized as an employer-employee relationship, then any work you create that is related to your employment or is created for the benefit of your employer will be considered work made for hire. This means your employer will be treated as the author of the work for copyright purposes. Second, if you are hired to work on someone else's work, it could be considered a work made for hire if you have entered into an agreement stating such and if the work falls into one of the nine categories set forth in the statute. In both of these instances, your copyrightable contributions to the work will be considered to be owned by the person paying you.

At this time, it is unclear if non-employee contributions to comic books fall under the work made for hire doctrine. If they do, it would be under the collective work provision, and this is the approach typically taken by the major publishers like DC and Marvel. The Act defines a collective work as "a work, such as a periodical issue, anthology, or encyclopedia, in which a number of contributions, constituting separate and independent works in themselves, are assembled into a collective whole." As you can see from this definition, it is possible the work someone contributes to a comic book might not fall under the work made for hire doctrine. In order to protect themselves and their intellectual property, the major publishers also include language in their agreements requiring freelancers to assign any and all rights they may have in contributions to the comic book to the publisher. While having freelancers sign an assignment provision is a good alternative solution in the event a freelancer's contributions are determined to not be a work made for hire, it is not ideal for the publisher. If the work is a work made for hire, then the publisher owns the copyright rights outright. However, if it is an assignment, then the Copyright Act has a provision that would allow creators to reclaim copyright assignments after 35 years.[85] This is what happened in the cases where Joe Simon sued Marvel over Captain America,[86] and the Siegel and Shuster heirs sued DC over Superman,[87] which we'll discuss in more detail later in the book. Obviously, publishers would prefer to prevent their rights to character from being terminated in the future.

If you want to create a comic book, then you also need to make sure you understand the work made for hire doctrine and use similar contracts as the major publishers do in order to protect your rights. For instance, if you want to hire a freelancer to work on your comic book, then you would need to have her sign a work made for hire agreement in order to prevent her from obtaining any copyright interests in your book. This agreement should state that she is entering a work made for hire agreement, and that all contributions she makes to the work will belong to you. Additionally, in order to further protect your work, it should also include language assigning all of her possible rights in her work to you. This should prevent the freelancer from unintentionally gaining a copyright interest in her contribution to your work. Obviously, if you want the freelancer to have a copyright interest in her contributions to your work, then a different contractual approach should be taken.

If you are being hired to work on someone's comic book, then the reverse of the above situation would apply. When you are hired to work on someone else's comic book, he should have you sign a contract. If he does not have you sign a work made for hire agreement, then you might be able to claim a copyright interest in your contributions to the work. If you do sign such an agreement, make sure you understand what it says and what, if any, rights you will be giving to him.

In order to better understand the two-pronged approach of claiming that something is a work made for hire and also having a freelancer assign her rights if it is not a work made for hire, I'm going to include a sample provision of this language as found in a publisher's work made for hire agreement. This example is over a decade old, but it is representative of what you will see if you are being hired to work on someone else's comic book. The work made for hire and assignment provision should look something like this:

> (A) The Work, including all preliminary materials and all results and proceeds thereof, has been specially commissioned by

[PUBLISHER] as "work made for hire," as such term is used in the United States Copyright Act of 1976. [PUBLISHER] shall have the right to alter and to engage others to alter the Work in any way, including by adding or deleting Pages at [PUBLISHER]'s sole discretion and without obligation to pay for any Pages or Cover Artwork beyond the number specified above.

(B) If [PUBLISHER] shall be deemed to not be the author and owner of the Work, then Talent irrevocably transfers and assigns to [PUBLISHER] all right, title, and interest in and to the Work, effective as of the creation thereof, for no additional consideration, including copyright and any renewals, extensions or revivals thereof, trademark rights and all other rights to exploit the Work in all media now or hereafter existing throughout the universe in perpetuity.

As you can see, the language needs to be broad in order to prevent a freelancer from acquiring any rights to her contributions to the work.

Archie Comics and the trouble it has had surrounding its *Sonic the Hedgehog* comics are a great example of what can happen when a publisher fails to include proper work made for hire language in its contracts. Archie Comics produces *Sonic the Hedgehog* comics under license from Sega, and it hired writers and artists to work on the comics.[88] A few years ago, one of the writers, Ken Penders, sued Archie over royalties and ownership for characters he created during his time working on the comics.[89] At the time he was hired, it appears that Archie failed to include language in its contracts declaring his work a work made for hire or otherwise assigning his creations to Archie.[90] This is a major problem for Archie. I have not seen the agreements between Sega and Archie or between Archie and Penders. However, it is typical in a license agreement to include language saying everything the licensee makes using the licensed property belongs to the licensor. Here Archie licensed from Sega the rights to make Sonic the Hedgehog comic books. Anything Archie made should ultimately belong to Sega, including new characters introduced. If Archie failed to pass on that contractual language to Penders, then they would be in breach of their agreement with Sega. In instances such as that, Sega could have terminated the contract, and Archie may have been obligated to pay monetary damages to Sega. Eventually, the parties settled.[91] Recently, another artist and writer who worked on the series has filed a similar lawsuit.[92] By failing to include the proper work made for hire language in its contracts, Archie lost the rights to use characters created for the *Sonic the Hedgehog* series, and it unnecessarily exposed itself to lawsuits. Archie also probably harmed its working relationship with Sega, from whom it was licensing the characters.

By understanding the work made for hire doctrine, you will be better positioned to protect your own creative works when you hire freelancers, and you will be able to understand what rights you are possibly giving away when you sign a work made for hire agreement.

iii.) Trademark

When starting your new business and comic, you might be creating trademarks. If you have adopted a business name, it also might be a trademark. For example, Marvel,[93] DC,[94] Image,[95] and Top Cow,[96] all are registered trademarks.

In addition to your business name, the title of the comics you are publishing may be entitled to trademark protection. As stated in the intellectual property overview section, titles of individual works generally are not subject to trademark protection, but if you are publishing an ongoing comic book series it might be entitled to trademark protection. Some recent examples of trademarked titles from Robert Kirkman's stable of comics include *The Walking Dead*,[97] *Thief of Thieves*,[98] and *Super Dinosaur*.[99]

If your comic becomes successful enough that you start to produce merchandise bearing your creations, then you may be able to register additional trademarks associated with those goods. See the discussion of the Superman examples in the intellectual property overview section on page 17.

As stated earlier, you may register a trademark with the USPTO at any time. Before you start publishing your comic, you may also file an intent-to-use application to reserve your rights to your prospective trademarks. You may file at any time after you have begun to use the trademark in commerce. Keep in mind, however, that federal trademark registrations can be costly. As of the time of writing, the filing fee per class of goods or services is $325 or higher, and there are additional fees for the renewals of your trademark.[100] Check the USPTO website for current fees. This is in addition to any attorney fees you may encounter, and if there are issues registering your trademark, the cost could escalate even higher.

iv.) Domains

Generally speaking, domain names are not considered intellectual property, but I believe they play an important role in today's intellectual property protection and enforcement strategies. In the "Clearance" section near the beginning of this book, I mentioned that you should check domain registries as part of your clearance search. This will help identify possible existing conflicts. At the same time, if you are committed to using the names you have selected for your comic book and your business, this is a great time to lock up those domains. Registering a domain is usually inexpensive, and you do not want someone else coming along later and registering a domain using the name of your comic or business. While it is possible to challenge a later registration, it can be costly and time-consuming, and it is not always possible to recapture a domain name. If you can afford to, it is best to spend the money early and secure the domain name rights to the names you are planning to use for your comic, character, and business.

v.) Using the DMCA Takedown Notice

Once you've started creating your comic book, it is possible that others might post it online without your consent. There are a few methods you can use to deal with these people, which I will touch on below, but my preferred method of removing online content that infringes on my client's work is the Digital Millennium Copyright Act ("DMCA") takedown notice. However, we will start by discussing some of the other approaches you can take.

Obviously, you can reach out to the person distributing your work online and ask them to take it down. Frequently, this will be enough, and it is an approach you can use in just about every instance where someone has posted your work online. The potential downside to this option is in how the person reacts. Sometimes, he will ignore you, and you'll have to resort to the options below. Sometimes, he will engage you in a conversation about what he has done and what you are doing, and this can be an opportunity to educate him about your work and your rights. Sometimes, however, he will be defensive and argue with you, which can be stressful and unproductive. Additionally, reaching out to people this way can be time consuming. Even with the downsides, this is still a good option in many cases. An unexpected benefit can occur when a person you've contacted about infringing your work will point out others who are also infringing your work, which reduces the time you have to spend seeking them out.

Another option, and the harshest, is to sue him. If someone is using or posting your work online without your permission, it is likely to be a copyright infringement. However, this can take a long time to wind through the courts, cost a lot of money up front, and, depending on the circumstances, it can make you look like a bully. Typically, this method would only be used as a last resort, or if the infringement is actually harming you financially.

My favorite option to remove infringing content from the internet is to send a DMCA takedown notice. Depending on where the work is posted, sending a DMCA takedown notice is the easiest way to enforce your rights. The DMCA was enacted in the late 1990s, and it includes a provision that limits online service providers' liabilities for copyright infringement if (i) they register with the Copyright Office a designated copyright agent to receive notice of infringement, (ii) they post the information on their website for the public to access, and (iii) they promptly respond to proper takedown requests sent to this copyright agent.[101] Online service providers are not required to take down material that is alleged to be infringing. However, if they receive a takedown notice and do not act, then they have been placed on notice of infringing materials, and they may face liability as a secondary infringer.[102] Due to the way this law is structured, online service providers almost always take down allegedly infringing material as soon as they are notified. Personally, I find this method to be one of the easiest ways to quickly remove infringing material from the internet, particularly if one website has a lot of infringing materials on it.

For example, if you are an online marketplace like Etsy where people are uploading and selling homemade items, you would not want to be held liable for copyright infringement for any infringing items being sold on your website by your users. So, you would register a copyright agent with the Copyright Office, usually someone in your legal department, and you would list the copyright agent's email address in an easily accessible area. If your copyright agent receives a proper takedown notice from someone who believes their copyrighted work is being infringed, and your website acts quickly to remove or disable the allegedly infringing content, then your website would not be found liable for secondary copyright infringement.

In order to send a DMCA takedown notice, you must send the following information in writing to the designated agent of the service provider:

(i) "A physical or electronic signature of a person authorized to act on behalf of the owner of an exclusive right that is allegedly infringed.
(ii) Identification of the copyrighted work claimed to have been infringed, or, if multiple copyrighted works at a single online site are covered by a single notification, a representative list of such works at that site.
(iii) Identification of the material that is claimed to be infringing or to be the subject of infringing activity and that is to be removed or access to which is to be disabled, and information

(iv) Information reasonably sufficient to permit the service provider to contact the complaining party, such as an address, telephone number, and, if available, an electronic mail address at which the complaining party may be contacted.

(v) A statement that the complaining party has a good faith belief that use of the material in the manner complained of is not authorized by the copyright owner, its agent, or the law.

(vi) A statement that the information in the notification is accurate, and under penalty of perjury, that the complaining party is authorized to act on behalf of the owner of an exclusive right that is allegedly infringed."[103]

Once you've sent a takedown notice containing all of the information above to the designated agent, a site will typically remove or disable the allegedly infringing material in a few days. The alleged infringer does have the ability to challenge your takedown and have the material reposted, but if it is clearly an infringement, they won't. The biggest downside to this method is it can sometimes feel like all you do is send DMCA takedown notices. The same material seems like it keeps reappearing in different places. Even though this can be frustrating, using the DMCA notice to remove infringing content online is still an easy and cheap method to protect your rights.

A typical DMCA takedown notice might look something like this:

My name is Dirk Vanover, and I am an attorney who writes original, copyrighted articles about the comics and entertainment industries at ComicsLawyer.com. It has come to my attention that at least one of my articles has been posted on your site without my permission.

My original article can be found here: [insert link].

The infringing article can be found here: [insert link]

I have a good faith belief that the use of the identified material in the manner complained of is not authorized by the copyright owner, its agent, or the law.

The information in the notification is accurate, and under penalty of perjury, I am authorized to act on behalf of the owner of an exclusive right that is allegedly infringed.

I look forward to your prompt compliance with this DMCA takedown notice as required by Section 512(c) of the Digital Millennium Copyright Act. Please contact me with any questions.

Sincerely,

Dirk Vanover
[Address]
[City, State, Zip]
(414) 465-8634
dirk@comicslawyer.com

The DMCA takedown notice is an effective and quick way to protect against the unauthorized distribution of your work online. Once you know how to use it, it might quickly become your favorite method of removing infringing material from websites.

c. The Infringement of Others' Intellectual Property

You've done your clearance search, and you've started your comic. You're in the clear, right? Not necessarily. Even though you may think you are in the clear, it is possible someone may believe you are infringing on his intellectual property. If this happens, you will most likely receive a cease and desist letter from an attorney threatening you with legal action and demanding you stop the infringing activity, provide an accounting of money earned, and all sorts of other nasty sounding language. It is important you do not ignore this letter. When you receive a cease and desist letter, immediately take it to your attorney who will be able to evaluate the merits of the demands being made and guide you in how to respond. Failing to take a cease and desist letter seriously could worsen the situation and escalate the problem.

Previously, I've mentioned and discussed a few notable cases from the comic book world, some of which involve infringement of intellectual property. We will round out this section by highlighting a few more lawsuits dealing with infringement of intellectual property that are interesting and informative.

The first two cases we will discuss both involve the right of publicity. The first case was tried in California and involves DC Comics and the singing duo the Winter brothers. In the 1990s, two new characters were introduced to the *Jonah Hex* miniseries named Johnny and Edgar Autumn.[104] The Autumn brothers were depicted with "pale faces and long white hair."[105] The Winter brothers, musicians known for their distinctive albino-like appearance, sued because they felt their names and likenesses were being used and falsely portrayed them as "'vile, depraved, stupid, cowardly, subhuman individuals who engage in wanton acts of violence, murder and bestiality for pleasure and who should be killed.'"[106] The court decided for DC Comics and found that the comics containing the Autumn brothers "do contain significant creative elements that transform them into something more than mere celebrity likenesses."[107] Our second case once again involves Todd McFarlane and was decided in Missouri at about the same time as the Winter brothers case. In McFarlane's *Spawn* comic book series, he introduced a character named Anthony "Tony Twist" Twistelli.[108] The *Spawn* character "is a Mafia don whose list of evil deeds includes multiple murders, abduction of children and sex with prostitutes."[109] In the letters columns of *Spawn* and in an interview in Wizard Magazine, McFarlane acknowledged that the "Tony Twist" character was named after the NHL player Anthony "Tony" Twist.[110] During trial, evidence was introduced that McFarlane marketed *Spawn* to hockey fans by producing "hockey pucks, hockey jerseys and toy zambonis" bearing the *Spawn* logo.[111] McFarlane "sponsored 'Spawn night' at a minor league hockey game, where McFarlane personally appeared and distributed Spawn products, including products containing the 'Tony Twist' character."[112] The court found that McFarlane's use of Tony Twist's name "was predominately a ploy to sell comic books and related products rather than artistic or literary expressions," and was therefore a violation of Twist's right of publicity.[113] After a second trial on these issues, a jury awarded Twist $15 million in damages.[114] It was later reported that the case was settled for $5 million.[115]

What can you take away from the Winter brothers and Tony Twist cases? Be careful when you choose to use someone's likeness in your comic. Even if you think it is a parody, entitled to fair use, or protected by the First Amendment, it could still lead to a long, costly legal battle with an outcome that can be very uncertain. As I stated before, the right of publicity varies from state to state, and the primary difference between the two outcomes in the cases above hinged on the tests the state courts decided to apply.

DC Comics was also sued for trademark infringement because of the origin story of their character Flex Mentallo. Charles Atlas, Ltd. ran well-known advertisements in comic books, including DC comic books, advertising their bodybuilding courses.[116] One of the well-known ads was a one-page comic strip story that shows a character named Mac being bullied.[117] Mac then takes the Atlas course, finds the bully and punches him, and "receives newfound respect, particularly from his female companion" and becomes the "hero of the beach."[118] In a 1992 issue of *Doom Patrol*, Flex Mentallo and his secret origin are introduced.[119] Mentallo's origin story "explicitly mirrors the storyline of plaintiff's comic ad."[120] The court noted that the story replicates key artwork and dialogue from the ad, and Mentallo wears swim trunks similar to those worn by Charles Atlas in his photographs that appear alongside the ad.[121] However, the comic continues by showing Flex Mentallo beating up the woman he was with and telling her "I don't need a tramp like you anymore!"[122] When the Charles Atlas company eventually discovered the character a number of years later, it sued DC.[123] At the time of the lawsuit, the comic book issue in question, *Doom Patrol* No. 42, had not been republished or redistributed since its initial publication.[124] However, the Flex Mentallo character did appear in some subsequent issues of *Doom Patrol* and a miniseries.[125] After it received a cease-and-desist letter from Charles Atlas' attorney, DC cancelled plans to distribute "a 1998 trade paperback that would have included the Flex Mentallo character[,]"[126] while also stating that there were "no present plans to reprint or redistribute any of the *Doom Patrol* issues in the *Flex Mentallo* series."[127] DC prevailed in the lawsuit on a number of different legal grounds, but Flex Mentallo was not used for a long time. However, in recent years, DC has republished the trade paperbacks of *Doom Patrol* and the *Flex Mentallo* miniseries.[128] DC also launched a new *Doom Patrol* title in late 2016, [129] in which the Flex Mentallo character reappears, almost two decades since his last appearance for DC.[130]

  Our lesson from the Flex Mentallo case: even if you think you are in the right, and you win your case, you still might be denied the use of a character you create if another person or entity believes it infringes their rights and is willing to sue over it. A court ruled the Flex Mentallo character to be protected under the First Amendment,[131] and it also found there was not a likelihood of confusion between the Flex Mentallo character and Atlas' ad.[132] However, one of the factors that seemed to sway the judge on the likelihood of confusion of the trademark claim was DC's representations "that it has no intention to use the Flex Mentallo character again[.]"[133] Additionally, one of the issues DC prevailed on was that Atlas waited too long to file the lawsuit, and the claims arising from *Doom Patrol* No. 42 were barred by the statute of limitations.[134] Based on the statute of limitations issue, republishing or reissuing this comic could give rise to a new claim for trademark infringement against DC. Even though DC won the case, it appeared hesitant to continue exploiting the character. We do not know if there was a settlement between the parties restricting DC's use of Flex Mentallo, or if DC was hesitant to use the character so as to avoid having to fight another lawsuit over Flex Mentallo. We do know that DC let twenty years pass before Flex Mentallo was set to reappear in an original comic book story after this lawsuit.[135]

  The final set of cases we'll discuss also involve DC Comics. However, this time they are the ones doing the suing. The first case is a precursor to the Captain Marvel case I discussed previously. In *Detective Comics, Inc. v. Bruns Publications, Inc., et al.*, DC sued Bruns because it believed its Wonder Man character infringed on DC's Superman copyrights.[136] The court found that Wonder Man did infringe on DC's copyrights due to the fact they are both "a man of miraculous strength and speed[,]" the "antics" of both characters are "closely similar[,]" each hides their identity "beneath ordinary clothing" and when removed stands in "skintight acrobatic costume[,]" each is shown crushing a gun in his hand, each is "termed the champion of the oppressed[,]" each is pictured stopping bullets, each are "endowed with sufficient strength to rip open a steel door[,]" and "[e]ach is described as being the strongest man in the world and each as battling against 'evil and injustice.'"[137] Of particular note in this case is the court's statement that even though Superman might be derivative of a Hercules, or other "heroes of literature and mythology[,]" since the Superman comics "embody an original arrangement of incidents and a pictorial and literary form" they are subject to copyright protection.[138] The court stated, "So far as the pictorial representations and verbal descriptions of 'Superman' are not a mere delineation of a benevolent Hercules, but embody an arrangement of incidents and literary expressions original with the author, they are proper subjects of copyright and susceptible of infringement because of the monopoly afforded by the act."[139] After winning this case and establishing their copyright interests in protecting Superman, and proving that a comic book character can be subject to copyright protection, DC initiated the lawsuit against Fawcett over Captain Marvel, as I discussed earlier. After their two successful attempts protecting their Superman copyrights in the '40s and '50s, DC tried again to sue under this theory in the '80s. They believed the television show *The Greatest American Hero* infringed on their copyrights to Superman.[140] Part of what appears to have prompted the dispute was that after the success of *Superman: The Movie*, ABC sought to license Superboy for a television series.[141] After failing to secure a license, ABC created a television series about a normal guy who becomes a superhero.[142] The television series "contain[ed] several visual effects and lines that inevitably call Superman to mind, sometimes by way of brief imitation, sometimes by mention of Superman or another character from the Superman works, and sometimes by humorous parodying or ironic twisting of well-known Superman phrases."[143] The character also had powers similar to Superman's.[144] However, the court found that the lead character in *The Greatest American Hero* did not infringe DC's right to Superman because the way he looks and acts "marks him as a different, non-infringing character who simply has some of the superhuman traits popularized by the Superman character and now widely shared within the superhero genre."[145]

Our lesson from the Wonder Man, Captain Marvel, and *The Greatest American Hero* cases: any similarities to an existing character could leave you susceptible to an infringement lawsuit. Personally, I believe over the years courts have become more adept at analyzing the differences and similarities between characters in a way that promotes creation, which partially explains the different outcomes DC obtained in the Wonder Man and Captain Marvel cases versus the result in *The Greatest American Hero* case.

d. Fan Art, Fair Use, and the First Amendment

Now that we've discussed many of the aspects of intellectual property protection and infringement, it is a good time to discuss fan art. It is fairly common for artists just starting out in the industry to attempt to show their skill and creativity by drawing images containing more popular characters owned by others. Many will also make prints of these drawings and sell them at conventions. Whenever I have hosted my *Comics Startup 101* panels at conventions and we start talking about intellectual property, the question of whether fan art is legal frequently comes up. The short answer, in my opinion, is no.

However, let's take a more nuanced look at the reasons why I feel this way. Just to make sure we are all on the same page, when I speak of fan art, I am talking about art, including fiction and other forms of expression, generated by a fan of a particular character, story, movie or other medium that is created without authorization from the owner of the property being depicted or from the person being depicted.

The three main areas of law that come into play when addressing fan art are copyright, trademark, and right of publicity. Since I have already discussed them more in-depth earlier in this book, I will not do so again here. However, to understand how copyright law applies to fan art I do need to state that part of the rights enjoyed by a copyright owner are the exclusive rights to reproduce his work[146] and to create derivative works based on his original work.[147]

Based on what we've discussed in the previous sections of this book about copyrights, trademarks, and right of publicity, I believe most fan art to be a violation of intellectual property laws. Typically, we have a fan creating an image of a popular character, such as Iron Man, without the permission of Marvel. Even though the fan's image may be distinct from other interpretations of Iron Man in the past, a copyright holder has the exclusive right to reproduce his works and to create derivative works. It is my belief that a fan creating an unauthorized Iron Man image is infringing on Marvel's copyright rights. Even if the fan is not selling copies of the fan art for profit, he might be violating Marvel's copyrights. The question of whether something constitutes copyright infringement does not solely rely on someone making a profit off of the infringement. Additionally, because

Marvel licenses Iron Man's image for use on merchandise, the fan could be in violation of Marvel's trademark rights. However, if the fan is selling copies of his art, then the question of whether it infringes Marvel's rights is even easier to decide in Marvel's favor. The right of publicity comes into play if this fan art is of Robert Downey, Jr.'s Iron Man. Not only would the fan be in violation of Marvel's intellectual property rights, he could also be in violation of RDJ's right of publicity.

If you're going to create fan art, then you should tread carefully. In all likelihood, drawing an image of your favorite character and posting it online will not get you sued. It's generally not in large media companies' interests to go after fans. Hopefully, the strongest response you might get is a request to remove the image. However, if you are creating unlicensed fan art and selling it online or at conventions, the risk of being noticed and getting into legal trouble increases greatly.

You might be asking, "What about fair use?" It is true that fair use is a limitation on a copyright holder's exclusive rights. If a work of art qualifies for the fair use exception, then it is found to not infringe another's copyrighted material. The language of the statute reads:

"...[T]he fair use of a copyrighted work, including such use by reproduction in copies or phonorecords or by any other means specified by that section, for purposes such as criticism, comment, news reporting, teaching (including multiple copies for classroom use), scholarship, or research, is not an infringement of copyright. In determining whether the use made of a work in any particular case is a fair use the factors to be considered shall include—
(1) the purpose and character of the use, including whether such use is of a commercial nature or is for nonprofit educational purposes;
(2) the nature of the copyrighted work;
(3) the amount and substantiality of the portion used in relation to the copyrighted work as a whole; and
(4) the effect of the use upon the potential market for or value of the copyrighted work.
The fact that a work is unpublished shall not itself bar a finding of fair use if such finding is made upon consideration of all the above factors."[148]

In addition to what is listed in the statute, the Supreme Court has also recognized parody as entitled to claim fair use because "it can provide a social benefit, by shedding light on an earlier work, and, in the process, creating a new one."[149] The court defined parody as a work that uses "some elements of a prior author's composition to create a new one that, at least in part, comments on that author's work."[150] Even though parody is entitled to a fair use defense, the court pointed out such a finding should not be presumptive, and a case of parody should be evaluated on a case-by-case basis through the application of the statutory factors.[151]

Fair use is a strong defense against a copyright infringement claim. However, you may have to go to court to assert it, which could be costly, and since it is judged on a case-by-case basis, it is not always consistently applied, which makes it difficult to predict an outcome. Relying on fair use to save you is a risky proposition.

There are not a lot of cases directly related to fan art. While lawsuits have been filed over fan created works, they rarely go to trial or reach a decision on the merits of the case. However, there are a few examples that might prove useful, particularly a trilogy of artistic cases.

The first case involves an artist making and selling prints of The Three Stooges. Gary Saderup was an artist who created charcoal drawings of celebrities, which he then would use on prints and t-shirts.[152] He sold lithographs and t-shirts with the images of The Three Stooges on them, and he did not have the consent of the company owning all rights to The Three Stooges, Comedy III Productions.[153] Saderup's profits from the sales of The Three Stooges merchandise was $75,000.[154] Comedy III Productions sued claiming his work violated The Three Stooges' publicity rights under California law.[155] In evaluating the case and determining the interplay between The Three Stooges' right of publicity and Saderup's First Amendment rights, the court adopted a "balancing test between the First Amendment and the right of publicity based on whether the work in question adds significant creative elements so as to be transformed into something more than a mere celebrity likeness or imitation."[156] In regards to Saderup, the court concluded "that depictions of celebrities amounting to little more than the appropriation of the celebrity's economic value are not protected expression under the First Amendment."[157]

A case similar to The Three Stooges case with a different outcome for the artist involves a painting of Tiger Woods. In this case, an artist painted scenes commemorating Woods' 1997 Masters Tournament victory and included the likenesses of former Masters winners looking down upon Woods.[158] Jireh, the artist's publisher, produced 250 serigraphs and 5,000 lithographs of the work to be sold at $700 and $100, respectively.[159] Woods sued for trademark infringement, violations of his right of publicity under Ohio law, and a number of other claims.[160] The court found Jireh's use of Tiger Woods' name in describing the painting was a fair use and did not violate his trademark right in his name because it was used in a purely descriptive manner.[161] The court also found the work did not violate Woods' right of publicity because it "has substantial informational and creative content," and it is entitled to First Amendment protection.[162] The court went on to compare this case to The Three Stooges case, and it found the art at issue here contains "significant transformative elements" as opposed to the "unadorned, nearly photographic reproductions of the faces of The Three Stooges."[163]

Rounding out our trilogy of artistic cases, we have an artist who painted images depicting famous scenes from University of Alabama football. Moore painted historical football scenes of Alabama football for decades.[164] At various times, he did so with a license from the University.[165] However, he eventually decided to stop seeking a license because he felt it was unnecessary to do so in order to recreate historic events.[166] Alabama eventually sued Moore for trademark infringement because he depicted the University's uniforms in paintings, prints, and calendars.[167] The court ruled that Moore's use "of the University's uniforms in the content of these items is artistically relevant to the expressive underlying works because the uniforms' colors and designs are needed for a realistic portrayal of famous scenes from Alabama football history[,]" does not infringe on Alabama's trademarks, and is protected by the First Amendment.[168] There are other elements to this case I am not discussing here for brevity's sake, but I do not believe they significantly impact the decision and the conclusions you can draw from it.

Another instructive case involves someone creating an encyclopedia of J.K. Rowling's *Harry Potter* universe. A fan created a website "that collected and organized information from the *Harry Potter* books in one central source for fans to use for reference."[169] The Lexicon website drew a significant amount of its encyclopedia content primarily from the *Harry Potter* series and companion books.[170] The creator of the site even received positive feedback from Rowling and her publishers about the site's value as a reference source.[171] Eventually, the creator of the site entered into a deal with a book publisher to turn elements of his site into a published encyclopedia, even though they were aware of Rowling's plans to do something similar.[172] Warner Bros. and Rowling sued for copyright infringement.[173] In evaluating the case, the court found that the book constituted copyright infringement,[174] and, after evaluating the statutory factors of fair use, it also found that the Lexicon was not entitled to a fair use defense because it was not "consistently transformative."[175] The judge ruled the Lexicon took "more of the copyrighted works than is reasonably necessary in relation to the Lexicon's purpose."[176] However, the court did rule that the Lexicon was not a derivative work,[177] and it stated "reference guides to works of literature should generally be encouraged by copyright law as they provide a benefit [to] readers and students; but…they should not be permitted to 'plunder' the works of original authors…'without paying the customary price[,]' lest original authors lost incentive to create new works that will also benefit the public interest.(internal citations omitted)"[178] The court prevented publication of the book and awarded Warner Bros. and Rowling statutory damages of $6,750,000.[179]

As I stated earlier, fair use is a defense to copyright infringement, but you will likely have to go to court to exercise that defense. At one time, the Lexicon was embraced by and used by Rowling and Warner Bros. However, as soon as it was going to be commercialized through publication, which was likely to conflict with Rowling's own encyclopedia, it became a threat. Eventually, a revised version of the book was released that closely followed the judge's guidelines from the lawsuit.[180]

The final case we'll discuss involves a copyright lawsuit over a Superman story submission. From a legal perspective, this case has limited value since it was never officially published, which means other courts do not have to follow the precedent it set. However, from a factual perspective, this case is too relevant to our discussion of fan art to ignore.

Marcel Walker submitted to DC Comics an Elseworlds story idea called "Superman: Last Son of Earth" reversing the traditional sequence of his origin so he is born on Earth and sent to Krypton.[181] Three years later, DC published a story with the same title and general plot idea, but different in "details and thrust of the stories."[182] DC argued that Walker's "springboard" submission was an unauthorized derivative work and could not be protected by copyright law, and the court agreed.[183] Walker acknowledged his submission as a derivative work but argued he was entitled to copyright protection because "DC granted him permission to use its copyright or that his 'springboard' was a 'fair use[,]'" and he was "entitled to copyright protection for whatever original elements he contributed to the derivative work."[184] In evaluating Walker's claims, the court found the submission guidelines Walker relied on in his argument did not grant him a "license to create derivative works or authorization to use DC's copyright-protected material."[185] It also ruled the Copyright Act's definition of fair use is inapplicable to the facts of the case, and it suggests Walker is confusing the legal term "fair use" with authorization and license.[186] Finally, the court found Walker was not entitled to copyright protection in his derivative work for any original elements he added to the story because he infringed DC's copyright in order to create it.[187] Quoting another case from the Third Circuit Court of Appeals, the court said "'if the underlying work is itself protected by copyright, then he will receive no protection at all; on the contrary, he is a copyright infringer, because in order to create his work he has copied the underlying work.'"[188]

So, is fan art legal? If your work qualifies for fair use under the Copyright Act and doesn't infringe on any trademark or right of publicity rights, then it might be. However, your typical artist alley renderings of Iron Man, Benedict Cumberbatch's Sherlock Holmes, or all of the Doctors are most likely going to be found to be an infringement. Draw carefully.

V. Who Owns Superman?

Superman has come up a number of times already in this book because DC has been aggressive in protecting its rights to the character. As such, any book discussing the law and comic books should at least mention the saga over the battle for the ownership rights to Superman. Earlier, I mentioned the dispute while discussing work-for-hire agreements and the termination of copyright transfers. The story of the ownership dispute between the creators of Superman and DC is long and complicated. There is a lot of information out there about it, and there are a lot of opinions. What follows is an attempt to present the facts as laid out in court decisions over the years.

Most people who've been around comics long enough know the story. Jerry Siegel came up with the basic idea of the Superman story in 1933, and he and Joseph Shuster created several weeks' worth of material for a possible comic strip.[189] They shopped the story for a number of years without finding a publisher.[190] Eventually, they started working on some comic strips for Detective Comics,[i] and, in 1938 DC decided to finally publish Siegel and Shuster's Superman story in its new book, *Action Comics*.[191] The two had already signed employment agreements stating DC owned all rights to the creations they made during their term of employment. On March 1, 1938, DC also had them execute an agreement giving all rights in the Superman strips to DC.[192] For the assignment of their rights to Superman, Siegel and Shuster received $130 as compensation from DC.[193]

In September 1938, they again executed another employment agreement with DC.[194] The agreement was to run for five years, and they were to be paid $10 per page for their work on Superman, in addition to being paid for their work on other comic strips at a lower rate.[195] It also reiterated that DC was the owner of all rights in the Superman strips.[196] By 1947, Siegel and Shuster's total compensation for the Superman strip was greater than $400,000.[197]

Also included in the employment agreement Siegel and Shuster signed with DC was a provision giving DC a right of first refusal to new stories they developed.[198] Around December 1938 and in December 1940, Siegel submitted detailed pitches for a Superboy comic.[199] In both cases, DC declined to publish it.[200] However, in 1944 while Siegel was stationed abroad during World War II, DC published a Superboy comic strip without

---

[i] Note: All references to DC may also refer to its parent companies, Warner Bros. or Time Warner. Due to the complications of corporate ownership, I will attempt to simplify things by referring to DC only unless necessary.

his knowledge or consent.[201] It also obtained a copyright registration in all materials in the magazine containing the Superboy strip.[202]

In 1947, Siegel and Shuster filed a lawsuit in New York against National Periodical Publications, the successor of DC. At issue in the case was whether the original agreement assigning Superman to DC was valid and whether DC violated Siegel's rights by publishing Superboy comics.[203]

In the case, Siegel and Shuster argued their previous agreements with DC should be "void for lack of mutuality and consideration."[204] In effect, they argued the compensation DC gave them for Superman was inadequate, and it rendered the agreement void. They also raised a whole host of arguments relating to DC's publication of Superboy without Siegel's knowledge or consent, and its attribution of the character to him.[205]

The court found the original assignment of the rights to Superman to DC "was valid and supported by consideration, and that, therefore, Detective was the exclusive owner of 'all' the rights to Superman."[206] The court also found that Superboy was Siegel's creation and a distinct work from Superman, and due to DC's failure to exercise its right of first refusal, Superboy belonged to Siegel.[207] Therefore, DC had "acted illegally."[208]

Both sides filed an appeal, but while it was pending, they reached an agreement on a settlement in 1948.[209] Siegel and Shuster received a payment of over $94,000.[210] Detective was again declared the sole owner of the rights to Superman, and it also received all ownership rights to Superboy.[211]

In the late 1960s and mid-1970s, Siegel and Shuster and Detective Comics again went to court over the ownership rights of Superman. At issue between the parties were the copyright renewal rights to Superman. Before I discuss the cases, I need to provide a brief overview of relevant copyright law at the time.

At the time of Superman's creation and at the time of the litigation, U.S. copyright law was governed by the Copyright Act of 1909. Unlike today where the full term of copyright protection is granted upon completion of a work, the original term of copyright protection was for 28 years from the date of publication.[212] The term of protection could be extended for an additional 28 years if a notice of renewal was filed with the copyright office.[213] The applicability of the work made for hire doctrine also was different than today (see Chapter 4 for more on the work made for hire doctrine). Even though the work made for hire doctrine was mentioned in the Copyright Act, there was no guidance provided.[214] Instead, courts applied various tests to determine whether an employee-employer relationship existed thereby making something a work made for hire.

After agreeing to settle the previous case over Superman and granting the rights to DC, Siegel and Shuster used the expiration of

Superman's initial copyright term and upcoming copyright renewal term in another attempt to regain control of the character they created. They filed their case in federal court in New York in 1969 seeking a declaration that they did not transfer the copyright renewal rights to DC.[215]

DC argued Siegel and Shuster had assigned the renewal rights to DC in the various agreements they had signed over the years and while settling the previous lawsuit.[216] DC also argued Superman was a work for hire and ownership of the character belonged to DC.[217]

The court ruled Siegel and Shuster were prevented from arguing many of their claims because of the previous settlement agreement.[218] It also ruled the language of the settlement agreement seemed to clearly state that Siegel and Shuster had transferred all ownership rights to DC, including the renewal rights.[219] Furthermore, the court ruled Superman was a work for hire because DC had instructed Siegel and Shuster on the revision and expansion of the Superman story published in *Action Comics* No. 1.[220]

On appeal, the Second Circuit court of appeals found the lower court had properly ruled that Siegel and Shuster were barred from relitigating the ownership of Superman due to the state court judgment in the 1948 case, and it found the lower court was correct in finding that the judgment and other agreements between the parties had transferred the copyright renewal rights to DC.[221] However, the Second Circuit did overturn the lower court's finding that Superman was a work for hire.[222]

After the '70s litigation, *The New York Times* featured a story depicting the current living conditions of the creators of Superman.[223] The story described them as nearly destitute and struggling to get by while their creation had earned millions for DC.[224] In the article, an executive vice president of Warner Communications, the parent company of DC, said that even though DC did not have a legal obligation to do anything for Siegel and Shuster, there was a moral obligation, and he said the company intended to provide them with an annual stipend.[225]

Following the article, and other ones like it, on Dec. 23, 1975, DC entered into another agreement with Siegel and Shuster.[226] Once again, Siegel and Shuster acknowledged that DC owned all rights to Superman.[227] In return, DC paid them "modest annual payments for the remainder of their lives; provided them medical insurance under the plan for its employees; and credited them as the 'creators of Superman.'"[228] The agreement gave each a lump sum of $17,500 and annual stipends of $20,000.[229] It was later raised to $30,000 per year, and they also received a $15,000 bonus after the success of *Superman: The Movie*.[230]

The agreement stated that DC was under no legal obligation to provide them with these payments. However, they were doing so because of their past contributions to the company and their current circumstances.[231] The agreement also stated DC would stop making the payments if either Siegel or Shuster, or someone on their behalf, asserted any rights to Superman.[232]

The agreement also provided Siegel's spouse with monthly payments for her life if Siegel died before Dec. 31, 1985. During the term of the agreement, DC "increased the amount of the annual payments, and on at least two occasions paid the pair special bonuses."[233] DC later amended the agreement with Siegel providing that his wife would continue to get his benefits if he predeceased her at any time.[234]

After Shuster died in 1992, DC increased the annual payments made to his sister to $25,000 per year, which she shared with her brother, and it paid all of Shuster's outstanding debt.[235] Shuster's sister and brother entered an agreement on October 2, 1992 confirming the above and regranting all of "Shuster's rights to DC and vowed never to assert a claim to such rights."[236] DC also paid her bonuses from time to time over the next few years ranging from $10,000 to $25,000.[237]

All told, DC paid the Siegels and Shusters more than $4 million under the 1975 agreement, as a later court found.[238]

During the same time as the 1975 agreement was being signed, Congress was revamping the Copyright Act. In 1976, a new Copyright Act was passed. Notably, it extended the duration of copyright terms and eliminated the copyright renewal term. Most important to our discussion here, it also gave artists the ability to terminate any previous transfers of their rights to their creations executed before January 1, 1978,[239] which was later extended to heirs in the '90s.[240] However, the termination provision would not apply to works made for hire.[241]

Had the Second Circuit upheld the decision that Superman was a work made for hire, the litigation between the DC and Superman's creators would have ended. However, the court's ruling that Superman was created by Siegel and Shuster and the change in copyright law opened the door for more litigation.

In 1997, Siegel's heirs, his widow and daughter, sent notices of termination to DC in an attempt to terminate the transfer of numerous works relating to Superman.[242] The termination date was listed as April 16, 1999.[243] As a court noted, "A flurry of settlement discussions between the parties quickly ensued, but just as quickly fizzled out. Nearly two years then passed without much discussion between the parties."[244]

The day before the termination date DC sent a letter to Siegel's attorney denying "'the validity and scope' of the termination notices."[245] The parties then reentered into settlement negotiations and signed an agreement to delay taking action on the termination notices as long as the agreement was in effect and the parties were attempting to resolve the matter.[246]

In October 2001, the attorney for the Siegel heirs sent a letter to DC setting forth an outline of a settlement agreement the parties had reached. Terms of the settlement, which also included rights to Superboy, called for the Siegel heirs to receive "a $2 million advance, a $1 million non-recoupable signing bonus, forgiveness of a previous $250,000 advance, a guarantee of $500,000 per year for 10 years, a 6% royalty of gross revenues, and various other royalties."[247]

A week later, DC's general counsel sent back "'a more fulsome outline'" of what DC believed they had agreed to and stated they were also working on a more detailed draft of the agreement.[248] In February 2002, DC's outside counsel sent over a 56-page draft agreement for the Siegel heirs to review.[249] This prompted Siegel's widow to write a letter to Time Warner's chief operating officer in May 2002 in which she said she felt "'stabbed in the back'" by "'new, outrageous demands.'"[250] She concluded by stating that after four years of negotiating, the parties had failed to reach a deal, and it was unlikely there would ever be a deal based on the contract sent to them.[251] Siegel's letter prompted Time Warner's CEO to respond that they didn't expect the agreement to be the final one and negotiations would continue on it, the company felt the main points previously agreed to were in the agreement, and DC still believed an agreement could be reached based upon the previously agreed to negotiations.[252]

The Siegel heirs rejected a redrafted agreement submitted to them by their attorneys in September 2002, fired their attorneys, and sent a letter to DC's president and publisher ending all negotiations with DC and its parent companies over the rights to Superman.[253] In October 2004, the Siegel heirs filed a lawsuit seeking to enforce their termination rights to Superman with help from their new attorney, Marc Toberoff.[254][ii]

[ii] Running alongside the dispute between the Siegel heirs and DC, was another dispute between DC and Toberoff. During the litigation, documents were taken from Toberoff's office and anonymously delivered to DC. *Pac. Pictures Corp. v. U.S. Dist. Court for Cent. Dist. Of Cal., L.A.*, 679 F.3d 1121, 1123-24 (9th Cir. 2012). These documents reportedly showed Toberoff approached the heirs while they were negotiating with DC, and offered to buy their rights to Superman. *DC Comics v. Pac. Pictures Corp.*, 938 F.Supp.2d 941, 946. (C.D. Cal. 2013). Shortly after the Siegel heirs stopped negotiating with DC, they signed an agreement with Toberoff to market and exploit their rights to Superman. *Id.* at 953. DC sued Toberoff and the related business entities involved in the deal for interfering with contractual relations between DC and the Siegel and Shuster heirs, amongst other claims. *Id.* at 947. A court ruled DC waited too long to bring the interference with contractual relations claims and was barred by the statute of

After settlement talks broke down between the Siegel heirs and DC, the Siegel heirs went to court to reclaim ownership of Superman. Initially, they met with success in their attempts. In 2008, a California federal district court ruled they had reclaimed Siegel's copyright interest in Superman and were a co-owner.[255] Later, the court limited the ruling to only apply to:

> (1) *Action Comics* No. 1 (subject to the limitations set forth in the Court's previous Order); (2) *Action Comics* No. 4; (3) *Superman* No. 1, pages three through six, and (4) the initial two weeks' worth of Superman daily newspaper strips. Ownership in the remainder of the Superman material at issue that was published from 1938 to 1943 remains solely with defendants.[256]

The family's victory, however, would be short-lived. DC appealed the district court's ruling to the Ninth Circuit, and in 2013 the Ninth Circuit ruled the 2001 agreement, discussed in the last post, was binding on the Siegel heirs, and therefore, DC retained ownership over Superman.[257] The court found, as a matter of California contract law, there was sufficient, definite terms outlining substantive payments to Siegel's heirs for there to be an agreed-upon contract.[258] The case was remanded to the district court, which upheld the ruling.[259] After the Ninth Circuit sent the case back to the district court, the Siegel heirs argued for the first time that Joanne Siegel had rescinded the 2001 agreement in written letters to DC, and DC did not object to the rescission.[260] The district court and the Ninth Circuit both rejected the newly raised argument because Joanne Siegel had passed away, and if the court allowed the Siegel heirs to raise these claims now the litigation would start all over again.[261]

As I mentioned previously, Shuster passed away in 1992, and he left behind his sister and brother as heirs. In 1992, they signed an agreement once again granting all of Shuster's rights in Superman to DC. After another change in the law allowed Shuster's estate to seek termination of the transfer of copyright, his family sought to do so, and in 2012, the Ninth Circuit ruled the 1992 agreement between DC and Shuster's heirs gave DC ownership of Shuster's interest in Superman.[262]

The first litigation involving the ownership of Superman occurred in 1947 and was resolved via a settlement. After another round of litigation, it looked like the ownership of Superman was settled in 1974. However, a change in the law gave Siegel and Shuster's heirs another chance to reclaim their creation. In 2016, it appears as if the dispute has

---

limitations. *Id.* at 955.

finally been resolved. DC owns the rights to Superman. Along the way, however, Siegel and Shuster, and their heirs, received substantive payments from DC.

Most people would agree Siegel and Shuster made a bad business deal when they initially transferred their rights to Superman for $130 in 1938. However, that was not the end of the story. They continued working on, and getting paid for, Superman stories for a decade thereafter. During their lifetimes, they sued DC twice. After the first lawsuit, they received a settlement payment. After the second, DC decided to pay them a bonus and annual payments, which were extended to their heirs. Their heirs and estates sued DC again after they passed away.

Personally, I've gone back-and-forth in my thoughts on this issue. I used to believe, as many do, that Siegel and Shuster were screwed over by DC. I've also thought DC was always within their legal rights in everything they did. The true answer lies somewhere in the middle. DC could have, and should have, responded to and treated Siegel and Shuster better during their lifetimes when they fell on hard times, even though DC had no legal obligation to do so. Also, even though they made a bad deal initially, Siegel and Shuster had plenty of opportunities to remedy the situation. Eventually, after years of litigation, I hope both sides realize that Superman would not have enjoyed as much success as he did, and would not be as valuable as he is, without the other side. Barring any changes in the law, it appears the battle over the rights to Superman has ended.

What are the lessons you can take away from this story? The most important lesson is to make sure you know what you are signing away in a deal. Siegel and Shuster might not have known at the time they signed the agreement and cashed the check that they were transferring to DC all of their rights to the character Superman. However, the language in the contract seems to clearly indicate that was the case. Additionally, have an idea of the value of the thing you're selling or transferring. No one could have guessed the wild success of the Superman character back when DC started publishing it. However, it is important to know what value you place on your creations, what you can achieve on your own, and what value others can bring to, or achieve with, your work. Additionally, as was evidenced over the years of struggle, make sure you know your rights so you can enforce them. It's hard to recover from a bad deal, but there are ways to do so, and occasionally the law is on your side. Finally, while it is always best to use contracts to protect yourself, someone still might sue you if they believe they are on the receiving end of a bad deal.

VI. Putting it Together – A Contract Walk Through

Now that we've talked about the importance of using contracts to protect yourself and your intellectual property, and we've discussed more in-depth the work made for hire doctrine, it might be helpful to walk through the major provisions of a contract. The contract we'll be discussing can be found in its entirety in Appendix A. It is a work made for hire agreement where an author is hiring an artist to create pages for his comic book.

This particular agreement is four pages long, and it includes a schedule attached to it. For the most part, the schedule is where the main deal points of the agreement will be memorialized. This is where the author will describe what the artist will be providing under the terms of the agreement, the submission timeline the artist will need to follow, and the amount the author will be paying the artist. Schedule A is the first place negotiations should start between the author and the artist addressing the work to be done, the compensation to be paid, the relevant time frames for completing the work, and any other pertinent deal points. The corresponding sections from the main body of the contract are set forth below.

1. SCOPE OF WORK

The Author desires to utilize the specialized skills, talents and other expertise of the Artist to perform certain services and tasks as set forth below. The completed results and product of Artist's services shall be deemed the "Work." The Work is specially ordered and commissioned by Author for use in connection with the [insert type of work] tentatively titled: [insert title]. The Work to be performed by Artist is set forth in Schedule A.

2. DELIVERY REQUIREMENTS

Artist will deliver to the Author the completed Work in form and content satisfactory to the Author according to the terms set forth in Schedule A. All work will be done in a competent and workmanlike fashion in accordance with applicable standards of the profession and all services are subject to final approval by Author prior to payment. Artist reserves the right to adjust the schedule in the event that Author fails to meet agreed upon deadlines for approval or payment and for more than customary changes and additions to the agreed upon scope of services. If Artist fails or refuses to meet the delivery requirements, Author may, at its sole election, terminate and cancel the applicable project or this Agreement in its entirety immediately. In either event, Author shall be released and discharged of and from any further obligations to Artist hereunder or otherwise with respect to the applicable project, including, but not limited to, the obligation to make any further payment to Artist for such project except for materials delivered and/or services rendered prior to such termination.

3. PAYMENT TERMS

In consideration for the services to be performed by Artist and upon acceptance of the Work, Author agrees to as set forth in Schedule A.

Sections 1 and 3 basically state that both parties agree to the terms set forth in the schedule. Section 2 states the same thing, but it also allows the artist some flexibility in changing the delivery schedule, and it also gives the author the ability to terminate the agreement if the artist fails to meet the delivery schedule. Of these three sections, only section two is likely to be negotiated between the parties. An artist might not be comfortable with the language allowing for termination at the author's discretion.

We are going to skip reviewing the language of section 4 because it is just dealing with whether or not the author will compensate the artist for expenses. In this case, and in most instances, the answer is no. However, if you choose to compensate the artist for some or all of their expenses, this will be the section in which to address it. It could also be set forth in the Schedule.

The next three sections focus on intellectual property.

5. COPYRIGHT OWNERSHIP

Artist acknowledges that the Work is being created by Artist for use in a Graphic Novel and that each form of Work is being created by Artist as a "work made for hire" under the United States Copyright Act and, at all stages of development, the Work shall be and remain the sole and exclusive property of the Author. At Author's sole, absolute and unfettered discretion, Author may make any changes in, deletions from, or additions to the Work. If for any reason the results and proceeds of Artist's services hereunder are determined at any time not to be a work made for hire, Artist hereby irrevocably transfers and assigns to Author all right, title and interest therein, including all copyrights and trademarks, as well as all renewals and extensions thereto. Artist irrevocably waives all rights of "droit morale" or "moral rights of authors" or any similar rights or principles of law that Artist may now or later have in the Work (whether now existing or hereinafter enacted). Artist acknowledges that Artist has entered into this Agreement before commencing the services hereunder. Artist further acknowledges that the Work commissioned hereunder may be derivative of preexisting material including, without limitation, the names, pictorial and literary representations of fictional characters, companies, places and things (the "Preexisting Material") that Author owns or otherwise has rights in the Preexisting Materials, and that Artist would be unable to produce the Work without the Preexisting Material and shall not have the right or privilege to use any of the Preexisting Material except as provided herein.

6. CREDIT

Nothing contained in this agreement shall be deemed to require the Author to use the Work, or any part thereof, in connection with the Graphic Novel or otherwise. Credit for the work shall read: [insert credit line], provided that a substantial portion of Artist's work is incorporated in the Graphic Novel. Author shall have sole responsibility in determining whether Artist is awarded sole, shared or no credit for the Work. No inadvertent failure by Author to comply with the credit line set forth above, nor any failure by third parties to so comply, shall constitute a breach of this agreement.

7. ARTWORK

Author shall return to Artist any original artwork created by Artist which was delivered to Author provided such original artwork shall have a stamp signifying that the copyright and all reproduction and distribution rights in and to such artwork belong to Author. If the original art is lost, or substantially damaged (in excess of the normal wear and tear sustained in publishing a comic publication), Author shall reimburse Artist an amount equal to the per page rate actually paid to Artist with respect to the lost or damaged original art, or if a page rate was not paid, an amount proportional to the amount actually received by Artist with respect to the lost or damaged original art.

As we discussed earlier, the work made for hire language is important in protecting intellectual property rights, and it is included here in section 5. Depending on the nature and intent of the relationship, this section can be negotiated. For instance, if you want to split the ownership of the comic book with the artist, you can change this section to explicitly state that the artist will be a co-creator. You could also choose to retain all rights to the work via the work made for hire provision but still grant the artist a percentage of the profits. This can be done in this section, or through adding language to the Schedule. However, if you do not want the artist to obtain any rights to your intellectual property, you should not agree to any changes you do not understand. The credit line and artwork sections can be negotiated and changed as needed. Other than possibly incurring additional expenses, these sections should not impact the author's rights.

The next three sections are not related to each other, but we will tackle them at one time for convenience.

8. INDEPENDENT CONTRACTOR

Artist is an independent contractor, not an employee. Artist is not eligible to participate in any pension, health, vacation pay, sick pay or other fringe benefit plan normally associated with an employee relationship. In addition, Artist will not be considered an employee with regard to any laws concerning Social Security, disability insurance, unemployment compensation, Federal, State or local income tax withholding at local source or any other laws, regulations or orders relating to employees. As such, Author will not withhold FICA or make FICA payments on Artist's behalf, make state or federal unemployment compensation contributions on Artist's behalf or withhold local, state or federal income tax from Artist's fees, and all such obligations shall be discharged by Artist as an independent contractor. Artist will indemnify Author against any claims, damages, liabilities and expenses of any kind arising out of or in connection with Artist's failure to discharge Artist's obligations as an independent contractor.

9. CANCELLATION

With reasonable cause, either party reserves the right to cancel this agreement without obligation by giving 30 days written notice to the other party of the intent to terminate. In the event that either party shall be in default of its material obligations under this agreement and shall fail to remedy such default within sixty (60) days after receipt of written notice thereof, this agreement shall terminate upon expiration of the sixty (60) day period.

10. PROMOTION
Artist hereby grants Author the right, but not the obligation, to use Artist's name, voice and approved likeness and approved biographical data in connection with the distribution, exhibition, advertising and exploitation of the [insert type of work].

Unless you are intending to hire the artist as an employee or take on responsibility for any employment-related issues, you should include language similar to that used in section 8 just to make clear the nature of the relationship. Generally speaking, this language is fairly common in independent contractor agreements of all types. The cancellation provision in Section 9 differs from many other agreements of this type. Typically, the ability to cancel only resides in one party, and in this situation it would reside with the author. However, this agreement allows for either party to terminate at any time on 30 days notice without reason. The language granting 60 days to a party to fix its breach of the agreement before termination is not unusual, and it is usually referred to as a cure provision. However, in this instance it is longer than the ability to terminate if there is no breach, which renders it somewhat pointless. This language would and should probably be modified during negotiations to address the discrepancy in the termination provisions. Generally, expect to negotiate the language regarding termination or cancellation of an agreement. It is usually a touchy subject, as no one wants to feel like they are going to get treated unfairly, but it is important to make sure it is clearly spelled out and agreed to by both parties. Likewise, the promotion language of section 10 can be negotiated, but most artists should not object to it. It would be difficult to promote and sell the book if you cannot talk about your co-contributors. However, the scope of the language and what permissions are being granted might be negotiated depending on the artist's comfort with promotional materials.

Of the remaining sections in the agreement, this one is the most likely to be a source of tension during negotiations.

11. ARTIST WARRANTIES AND REPRESENTATIONS, INDEMNIFICATION
Artist warrants and represents that he/she has the right to enter into this agreement and to grant Author all rights herein granted, and that Artist has not entered into or will enter into any agreement of any kind that will interfere in any way with the complete performance of this agreement. Except to the extent based on material provided by the Author to be used as the basis thereof, Artist warrants and represents that the Work (i) shall be wholly original with Artist, (ii) shall not infringe upon any copyright, trademark, the right of privacy or publicity or any other rights of any person or entity, and (ii) is not and shall not be the subject of any litigation or other proceeding or claim that might give rise to litigation or any other proceeding. Artist shall indemnify and hold harmless Author, its successors or assigns, from and against any and all liabilities, claims, suits, judgments, costs, or expenses

(including, without limitation, attorneys' fees and courts costs, whether or not in connection with litigation) arising from any breach of any of the covenants, representations and/or warranties made by Artist herein. Artist's warranties, representations and indemnity herein shall survive the expiration or termination of this Agreement.

Even though this language is fairly reasonable, some artists will push back against this provision. In this section, the artist is saying that he can enter into this agreement freely, i.e., he is not prohibited by contract or otherwise from doing so, that the work the artist is providing will be original, and that it will not violate the rights of any other person. The artist then agrees to indemnify and hold harmless the author from a breach of these warranties and representations. This indemnification language means that the artist would be responsible for paying the author's legal bills, judgments, damages, etc., if the author gets sued because of something the artist has done. Additionally, there is language included that makes this section survive any expiration or termination of the agreement. The artist's obligations under this section become indefinite. As you can imagine, the financial risk to the artist can be very high because of this language. If he includes something in the book, such as a logo or image, that infringes another's intellectual property rights, he could be responsible for all of the legal fees and damages if the author gets sued. Unless your indemnification language is very reasonable, expect most people to negotiate this section. However, be very careful if you make changes to this section. You want to protect yourself, and you do not want to expose yourself to unnecessary financial risks. It is also likely artists will want language added indemnifying them from any lawsuits that might arise from your instructions. Typically, this is a reasonable request, but you will want to gauge your risk. Care should be taken when drafting language that explicitly increases your financial risk under a contract.

Of the remaining sections of the contract, I am only going to talk in depth about one. The sections on amendments, severability, and notices are pretty standard and mostly harmless. The remaining section can be very important.

12. ASSIGNMENT, ENTIRETY OF AGREEMENT, GOVERNING LAW, JURISDICTION AND MEDIATION.
Artist may not assign, directly or indirectly, all or part of its rights or obligations under this agreement to any other person or entity without first obtaining the written permission of Author. This agreement constitutes the entire agreement between the parties. No modification shall be enforceable except in writing and signed by the parties hereto. This agreement shall be governed by the laws of the state of Illinois. In the event any dispute arising under this agreement results in litigation, arbitration, or mediation, such action or proceeding shall be brought within the state or federal courts of Illinois. Mediation of any dispute arising from this agreement shall be conducted in accordance with the rules of the Patricia Felch Arts Mediation Services, a program of the Lawyers for the Creative Arts.

The assignment language is standard and shouldn't be an issue. You are hiring the artist, not someone the artist chooses to finish the work. Additionally, you should note the language stating this is the complete agreement between the parties. This language means what it says. This contract, as written down, is the complete evidence of the agreement between the two parties. If there were any promises made that are not included in the contract, then they are not a part of the agreement. It is very difficult to enforce any promises made relating to a contract that are not actually a part of the contract. Make sure everything you want is in the agreement. Otherwise, you probably won't be able to enforce it if the other party doesn't deliver.

The main point of contention in this section will be the governing law and the jurisdiction. Different states have different laws, and the way states interpret and enforce contracts can vary greatly. Some care should be taken to decide which state's law you want to govern. Generally, most people choose the state where they are located, but some may prefer other states if they have more favorable laws governing their industry. Additionally, most people prefer to include where the parties must litigate any disputes that arise under the agreement. The person commissioning the work, here the author, will want it to be in his home state. Some artists may want to change the jurisdiction and venue, and you may want to accommodate them. However, any changes could be harmful to your ability to enforce the agreement. For instance, if you agree to jurisdiction and venue in the artist's state or in a neutral state, your costs of hiring an attorney and filing a lawsuit may increase. Changing the venue and jurisdiction may make you less inclined to enforce your rights. Additionally, some states have laws that might conflict with or be unfavorable to your business deal. If you choose to litigate in a state that looks unfavorably upon your deal, they may rule against you, even if the contract explicitly says another state's laws should apply. In addition to the jurisdiction provision, this contract also has a mediation provision. Typically, it's good to include one because mediation is less costly than litigation. Most people won't object to the idea of mediation or arbitration, but they may want to change the organization providing the service, the rules governing it, or the location where it takes place. As with jurisdiction and venue, be careful if you are contemplating making these changes and make sure you understand the costs and risks involved if you do so.

The contract we just looked at involved an author hiring an artist to work on the author's project. Even though it is missing some sections people might want to include, such as a confidentiality clause, it is a pretty good contract overall. If you are making your own comic book, you should be using an agreement similar to this one with every person you hire to work on your book. Using a contract will protect your intellectual property, and it will protect you in the event of a dispute with the people you hire. An attorney can be beneficial to use in the negotiation of these types of agreements. If you are not using an attorney, make sure you understand all of the provisions of the agreement, any changes made to the agreement, and how it impacts you.

VII. Conclusion

      I hope you enjoyed reading my book as much as I enjoyed writing it. Do not let anything contained in this book frighten you from making the comic book you want to make. The intent is not to frighten you, but to educate you about possible problems you might encounter. Even though I barely scratched the surface of the issues you will need to be aware of as you start your career, I believe I have given you a great base of knowledge from which to proceed forward.

      As you start your career making comics, keep in mind the topics and lessons I discussed. If you choose to start another type of business, the lessons learned here should still prove useful. These issues are universal to most businesses, and understanding them and learning from them will help keep you and your business out of trouble.

About the Author

Dirk Vanover is an attorney and the founder of Vanover Legal, LLC. His practice focuses on the areas of entertainment, intellectual property, and business law. He also writes about legal issues impacting the comic book and entertainment industries at ComicsLawyer.com.

Prior to founding his own solo practice, he worked as an associate general counsel for an online retailer of Halloween costumes and party supplies. He obtained his law degree from Marquette University Law School, and he holds a bachelor's and master's degree in journalism from the University of Illinois. He is licensed to practice law in Wisconsin and Illinois, and he lives in the Milwaukee area with his wife, daughter, and two cats.

Appendix A

WORK MADE FOR HIRE AGREEMENT

This work made for hire agreement is dated [month][day],[year] and is between [name], as purchaser of the Work ("Author"), and [name], as producer of the Work ("Artist")(the "Agreement").

1. SCOPE OF WORK

The Author desires to utilize the specialized skills, talents and other expertise of the Artist to perform certain services and tasks as set forth below. The completed results and product of Artist's services shall be deemed the "Work." The Work is specially ordered and commissioned by Author for use in connection with the [insert type of work] tentatively titled: [insert title]. The Work to be performed by Artist is set forth in Schedule A.

2. DELIVERY REQUIREMENTS

Artist will deliver to the Author the completed Work in form and content satisfactory to the Author according to the terms set forth in Schedule A. All work will be done in a competent and workmanlike fashion in accordance with applicable standards of the profession and all services are subject to final approval by Author prior to payment. Artist reserves the right to adjust the schedule in the event that Author fails to meet agreed upon deadlines for approval or payment and for more than customary changes and additions to the agreed upon scope of services. If Artist fails or refuses to meet the delivery requirements, Author may, at its sole election, terminate and cancel the applicable project or this Agreement in its entirety immediately. In either event, Author shall be released and discharged of and from any further obligations to Artist hereunder or otherwise with respect to the applicable project, including, but not limited to, the obligation to make any further payment to Artist for such project except for materials delivered and/or services rendered prior to such termination.

3. PAYMENT TERMS

In consideration for the services to be performed by Artist and upon acceptance of the Work, Author agrees to as set forth in Schedule A.

4. EXPENSES

Artist shall be responsible for all expenses incurred while performing services under this agreement.

5. COPYRIGHT OWNERSHIP

Artist acknowledges that the Work is being created by Artist for use in a Graphic Novel and that each form of Work is being created by Artist as a "work made for hire" under the United States Copyright Act and, at all stages of development, the Work shall be and remain the sole and exclusive property of the Author. At Author's sole, absolute and unfettered discretion, Author may make any changes in, deletions from, or additions to the Work. If for any reason the results and proceeds of Artist's services hereunder are determined at any time not to be a work made for hire, Artist hereby irrevocably transfers and assigns to Author all right, title and interest therein, including all copyrights and trademarks, as well as all renewals and extensions thereto. Artist irrevocably waives all rights of "droit morale" or "moral rights of authors" or any similar rights or principles of law that Artist may now or later have in the Work (whether now existing or hereinafter enacted). Artist acknowledges that Artist has entered into this Agreement before commencing the services hereunder. Artist further acknowledges that the Work commissioned hereunder may be derivative of preexisting material including, without limitation, the names, pictorial and literary representations of fictional characters, companies, places and things (the "Preexisting Material") that Author owns or otherwise has rights in the Preexisting Materials, and that Artist would be unable to produce the Work without the Preexisting Material and shall not have the right or privilege to use any of the Preexisting Material except as provided herein.

6. CREDIT

Nothing contained in this agreement shall be deemed to require the Author to use the Work, or any part thereof, in connection with the Graphic Novel or otherwise. Credit for the work shall read: [insert credit line], provided that a substantial portion of Artist's work is incorporated in the Graphic Novel. Author shall have sole responsibility in determining whether Artist is awarded sole, shared or no credit for the Work. No inadvertent failure by Author to comply with the credit line set forth above, nor any failure by third parties to so comply, shall constitute a breach of this agreement.

7. ARTWORK

Author shall return to Artist any original artwork created by Artist which was delivered to Author provided such original artwork shall have a stamp signifying that the copyright and all reproduction and distribution rights in and to such artwork belong to Author. If the original art is lost, or substantially damaged (in excess of the normal wear and tear sustained in publishing a comic publication), Author shall reimburse Artist an amount equal to the per page rate actually paid to Artist with respect to the lost or damaged original art, or if a page rate was not paid, an amount proportional to the amount actually received by Artist with respect to the lost or damaged original art.

8. INDEPENDENT CONTRACTOR

Artist is an independent contractor, not an employee. Artist is not eligible to participate in any pension, health, vacation pay, sick pay or other fringe benefit plan normally associated with an employee relationship. In addition, Artist will not be considered an employee with regard to any laws concerning Social Security, disability insurance, unemployment compensation, Federal, State or local income tax withholding at local source or any other laws, regulations or orders relating to employees. As such, Author will not withhold FICA or make FICA payments on Artist's behalf, make state or federal unemployment compensation contributions on Artist's behalf or withhold local, state or federal income tax from Artist's fees, and all such obligations shall be discharged by Artist as an independent contractor. Artist will indemnify Author against any claims, damages, liabilities and expenses of any kind arising out of or in connection with Artist's failure to discharge Artist's obligations as an independent contractor.

9. CANCELLATION

With reasonable cause, either party reserves the right to cancel this agreement without obligation by giving 30 days written notice to the other party of the intent to terminate. In the event that either party shall be in default of its material obligations under this agreement and shall fail to remedy such default within sixty (60) days after receipt of written notice thereof, this agreement shall terminate upon expiration of the sixty (60) day period.

10. PROMOTION

Artist hereby grants Author the right, but not the obligation, to use Artist's name, voice and approved likeness and approved biographical data in connection with the distribution, exhibition, advertising and exploitation of the [insert type of work].

11. ARTIST WARRANTIES AND REPRESENTATIONS, INDEMNIFICATION

Artist warrants and represents that he/she has the right to enter into this agreement and to grant Author all rights herein granted, and that Artist has not entered into or will enter into any agreement of any kind that will interfere in any way with the complete performance of this agreement. Except to the extent based on material provided by the Author to be used as the basis thereof, Artist warrants and represents that the Work (i) shall be wholly original with Artist, (ii) shall not infringe upon any copyright, trademark, the right of privacy or publicity or any other rights of any person or entity, and (ii) is not and shall not be the subject of any litigation or other proceeding or claim that might give rise to litigation or any other proceeding. Artist shall indemnify and hold harmless Author, its successors or assigns, from and against any and all liabilities, claims, suits, judgments, costs, or expenses (including, without limitation, attorneys' fees and courts costs, whether or not in connection with litigation) arising from any breach of any of the covenants, representations and/or warranties made by Artist herein. Artist's warranties, representations and indemnity herein shall survive the expiration or termination of this Agreement.

12. ASSIGNMENT, ENTIRETY OF AGREEMENT, GOVERNING LAW, JURISDICTION AND MEDIATION.

Artist may not assign, directly or indirectly, all or part of its rights or obligations under this agreement to any other person or entity without first obtaining the written permission of Author. This agreement constitutes the entire agreement between the parties. No modification shall be enforceable except in writing and signed by the parties hereto. This agreement shall be governed by the laws of the state of Illinois. In the event any dispute arising under this agreement results in litigation, arbitration, or mediation, such action or proceeding shall be brought within the state or federal courts of Illinois. Mediation of any dispute arising from this agreement shall be conducted in accordance with the rules of the Patricia Felch Arts Mediation Services, a program of the Lawyers for the Creative Arts.

13. AMENDMENTS

The written provisions contained in this Agreement constitute the sole and entire agreement made between Artist and Author concerning the Work, and any amendments to this Agreement shall not be valid unless made in writing and signed by both parties.

14. SEVERABILITY

If any provision of this agreement or the application thereof is held invalid, the invalidity shall not affect other provisions or applications of this agreement which can be given effect without the invalid provisions or application, and to this end the provisions of this agreement are declared to be severable.

15. NOTICES

All notices required to be sent under this Agreement shall be in writing and shall be sent to the address of the party below:

Name of
Artist:_____
Address:_____
City: _____ State: _____
Zip:_____
Telephone: _____
E-mail Address:_____

Author:_____
Address:_____
City: _____ State: _____
Zip:_____
Telephone:_____
E-mail Address:_____

Author   Artist
Signature:_____ Signature:_____
Printed Name:_____ Printed Name:_____
Date:_____ Date:_____

SCHEDULE A

Scope of Work
[insert detailed description of work artist will be performing]

Compensation
[insert description of artist's compensation and when it will be paid]

Delivery schedule
[insert time frame for delivery of work under the Agreement]

Endnotes

[1] National Comics Publications, Inc. v. Fawcett Publications, 93 F.Supp.349, 354 (S.D.N.Y. 1950).
[2] Vaneta Rogers, *Exclusive: Geoff Johns Hopes Lightning Strikes Shazam!*, Newsaram.com, Jan. 26, 2012, http://www.newsarama.com/8995-exclusive-geoff-johns-hopes-lightning-strikes-shazam.html (last visited January 25, 2017).
[3] National Comics Publications, Inc., 93 F.Supp.352 (S.D.N.Y. 1950).
[4] National Comics Publications, Inc. v. Fawcett Publications, Inc. et. al., 191 F.2d 594, 598 (2nd 1951).
[5] *Id.* at 597.
[6] *Id.*
[7] National Comics Publications, Inc., 93 F.Supp 355-56 (S.D.N.Y. 1950).
[8] Matt Lage (2001). "Visual Expression: Will Lieberson - Fawcett Comics Executive Editor". In Hamerlinck, P.C., *Fawcett Companion: The Best of FCA* (1st ed.). TwoMorrows Publishing. pp. 94–95.
[9] Mark Buxton, *The Rich History of Captain Mar...Er, Shazam!*, Comic Book Resources, Aug. 29, 2014, http://www.comicbookresources.com/?page=article&id=55178 (last visited January 25, 2017).
[10] *Id.*; *see also* Trad. Reg. No. 0976419, Registration Date Jan. 8, 1974.
[11] Small Business Administration, Limited Liability Company, https://www.sba.gov/starting-business/choose-your-business-structure/limited-liability-company (last visited January 25, 2017).
[12] *Id.*
[13] *Id.*
[14] *Id.*
[15] *Id.*
[16] *Id.*
[17] *Id.*
[18] Internal Revenue Service, Limited Liability Company, https://www.irs.gov/Businesses/Small-Businesses-&-Self-Employed/Limited-Liability-Company-LLC (last visited January 25, 2017).
[19] *Id.*
[20] Small Business Adminstration, Corporations, https://www.sba.gov/starting-business/choose-your-business-structure/corporation (last visited January 25, 2017).
[21] Small Business Adminstration, S Corporations, https://www.sba.gov/starting-business/choose-your-business-structure/s-corporation (last visited January 25, 2017).
[22] *Id.*
[23] *See* Internal Revenue Service, S Corporations, https://www.irs.gov/Businesses/Small-Businesses-&-Self-Employed/S-Corporations (last visited January 25, 2017).

[24] Small Business Adminstration, S Corporations, https://www.sba.gov/starting-business/choose-your-business-structure/s-corporation (last visited January 25, 2017).
[25] *Id.*
[26] Gaiman v. McFarlane, 360 F.3d 644 (7th Cir. 2004), at 649.
[27] Gaiman v. McFarlane, 360 F.3d 644 (7th Cir., 2004), at 649.
[28] Id at 651.
[29] *Id.* at 650.
[30] *Id.*
[31] *Id.* at 651.
[32] *Id.*
[33] *Id.* at 652.
[34] Id at 652.
[35] *Id.* at 648.
[36] Id at 657.
[37] Gaiman v. McFarlane (W.D. Wis. 2012).; Associated Press, Neil Gaiman, Todd McFarlane settle long-running Spawn lawsuit, CBC.com, Jan 31, 2012, http://www.cbc.ca/news/entertainment/neil-gaiman-todd-mcfarlane-settle-long-running-spawn-lawsuit-1.1277283 (last visited January 25, 2017).
[38] Geoff Boucher, *FIRST LOOK: Neil Gaiman's avenging Angela will make Marvel history*, EW.com, May 09, 2013, http://www.ew.com/article/2013/05/09/neil-gaiman-angela-age-of-ultron (last visited January 25, 2017).
[39] Matthew Belloni, *'Walking Dead' War: Creator Robert Kirkman sued by Collaborator*, HollywoodReporter.com, Feb. 09, 2012, http://www.hollywoodreporter.com/thr-esq/walking-dead-war-creator-robert-288671 (last visited January 25, 2017).
[40] Graeme McMillan, The Walking Dead *Behind-the-Scenes Battle that Almost Doubled the Zombie Count*, Time.com, Oct. 10, 2012, http://entertainment.time.com/2012/10/10/the-walking-dead-behind-the-scenes-battle-that-almost-doubled-the-zombie-count/ (last visited January 25, 2017).
[41] *Id.*
[42] *Id.*
[43] *Id.*
[44] Dave Itzikoff, *The Vendetta Behind 'V for Vendetta'*, NYTimes.com, Mar. 12, 2006, http://www.nytimes.com/2006/03/12/movies/12itzk.html?_r&_r=0 (last visited January 25, 2017).
[45] Circular 1, Copyright Basics, U.S. Copyright Office, http://www.copyright.gov/circs/circ01.pdf (last visited January 25, 2017).
[46] 17 U.S.C. §102(a).
[47] *Id.*
[48] 17 U.S.C. §302(a).
[49] Circular 15a, Duration of Copyright, 1, U.S. Copyright Office, http://www.copyright.gov/circs/circ15a.pdf (last visited January 25, 2017).
[50] 17 U.S.C. §107.

[51] 17 U.S.C. §408(a).
[52] 17 U.S.C. §407(a).
[53] U.S. Copyright Office, Copyright Basics, http://www.copyright.gov/circs/circ01.pdf (last visited January 25, 2017).
[54] *See Id.*
[55] What is a trademark?, United States Patent and Trademark Office, http://www.uspto.gov/learning-and-resources/trademark-faqs (last visited January 25, 2017).
[56] How long does a trademark registration last?, United States Patent and Trademark Office, http://www.uspto.gov/learning-and-resources/trademark-faqs (last visited January 25, 2017).
[57] Must I register my trademark?, United States Patent and Trademark Office, http://www.uspto.gov/learning-and-resources/trademark-faqs (last visited January 25, 2017).
[58] What are "common law" rights?, United States Patent and Trademark Office, http://www.uspto.gov/learning-and-resources/trademark-faqs (last visited January 25, 2017).
[59] What are the benefits of federal trademark registration?, United States Patent and Trademark Office, http://www.uspto.gov/learning-and-resources/trademark-faqs (last visited January 25, 2017).
[60] *See* What is "interstate commerce"?, United States Patent and Trademark Office, http://www.uspto.gov/learning-and-resources/trademark-faqs (last visited January 25, 2017).
[61] Trademark Manual of Examining Procedure, §1202.08 (April 2016).
[62] *Id.*
[63] *Id.*
[64] *In re Cooper*, 254 F.2d 611, 616 (C.C.P.A. 1958).
[65] *See* What is a copyright?, United States Patent and Trademark Office, http://www.uspto.gov/learning-and-resources/trademark-faqs (last visited January 25, 2017).
[66] Trad. Reg. No. 4656403, Registered Dec. 16, 2014.
[67] Trad. Reg. No. 2211378, Registered Dec. 15, 1998.
[68] *Id.*
[69] *Id.*
[70] Trad. Reg. No. 2226415, Registered Feb. 23, 1999.
[71] Trad. Reg. No. 1173150, Registered Oct. 13, 1981.
[72] Stacey L. Dogan & Mark A. Lemley, *What the Right of Publicity Can Learn from Trademark Law*, 58 Stanford Law Review 1161, 1167-73 (2006).
[73] Id at 1167-74.
[74] Id at 1174.
[75] *Id.*
[76] *Id.* At 1174-75 (internal citations omitted).
[77] 17 U.S.C. §102(a).
[78] Circular 1, Copyright Basics, 6, U.S. Copyright Office, http://www.copyright.gov/circs/circ01.pdf (last visited January 25, 2017).

[79] *Id.*
[80] *Id.*
[81] *Id.*
[82] 17 U.S.C. §504.
[83] 17 U.S.C. §101
[84] 17 U.S.C. §201(b).
[85] 17 U.S.C. §203
[86] *See* Marvel Characters, Inc. v. Joseph Simon, 310 F.3d 280 (2nd Cir. 2002).
[87] *See* Siegel v. Warner Bros. Ent., Inc., 542 F.Supp.2d 1098 (C.D. Cal. 2008).
[88] Rich Johnston, *Archie Desperate to Settle, but Can't Without Sega – The Latest in the Ken Penders Sonic Comics Case*, May 9, 2013, BleedingCool.com, http://www.bleedingcool.com/2013/05/09/archie-desperate-to-settle-but-cant-without-sega-the-latest-in-the-ken-penders-sonic-comics-case/ (last visited January 25, 2017).
[89] *Id.*
[90] Rich Johnston, *Now Scott Fulop Sues Archie Comics and Sega over Sonic the Hedgehog Characters*, Aug. 8, 2016, BleedingCool.com, http://www.bleedingcool.com/2016/08/08/now-scott-fulop-sues-archie-comics-and-sega-over-sonic-the-hedgehog-characters/ (last visited January 25, 2017).
[91] Rich Johnston, *Archie Comics Settles with Ken Penders Over Sonic the Hedgehog Lawsuit*, BleedingCool.com, http://www.bleedingcool.com/2013/07/11/archie-comics-settles-with-ken-penders-over-sonic-the-hedgehog-lawsuit/ (last visited January 25, 2017).
[92] Rich Johnston, *Now Scott Fulop Sues Archie Comics and Sega over Sonic the Hedgehog Characters*, Aug. 8, 2016, BleedingCool.com, http://www.bleedingcool.com/2016/08/08/now-scott-fulop-sues-archie-comics-and-sega-over-sonic-the-hedgehog-characters/ (last visited January 25, 2017).
[93] Trad. Reg. No. 0870506, Registered June 3, 1969.
[94] Trad. Reg. No. 1003409, Registered January 28, 1975.
[95] Trad. Reg. No. 1884871, Registered March 21, 1995.
[96] Trad. Reg. No. 2120058, Registered December 9, 1997.
[97] Trad. Reg. No. 4443715, Registered December 3, 2103.
[98] Trad. Reg. No. 4430107, Registered November 5, 2013.
[99] Trad. Reg. No. 4149779, Registered May 29, 2012.
[100] *See* Trademark Processing Fees, USPTO, http://www.uspto.gov/learning-and-resources/fees-and-payment/uspto-fee-schedule#TM%20Process%20Fee (last visited January 25, 2017).
[101] Online Service Providers, U.S. Copyright Office, http://www.copyright.gov/onlinesp/ (last visited January 25, 2017).
[102] *Id.*
[103] 17 U.S.C. §512(c)(3)(A)
[104] Winter v. DC Comics, 134 Cal.Rptr.2d 634, 637-38. (Cal. 2003).
[105] *Id.* at 637.
[106] *Id.* at 638.
[107] *Id.* at 637.

[108] Doe v. Tci Cablevision, 110 S.W.3d 363, 366 (Mo. 2003).
[109] *Id.*
[110] *Id.* at 366-67.
[111] *Id.* at 367.
[112] *Id.*
[113] *Id.* at 374.
[114] Doe v. McFarlane, 207 S.W.3d 52, 56 (Mo. App. 2006).
[115] ICv2.com, *'Twist Case Settled,'* Feb. 18, 2007, http://icv2.com/articles/comics/view/10104/twist-case-settled (last visited January 25, 2017).
[116] Charles Atlas, Ltd. v. DC Comics, Inc., 112 F.Supp.2d 330, 331-32.
[117] *Id.* at 331.
[118] *Id.*
[119] *Id.* at 332.
[120] *Id.*
[121] *Id.*
[122] *Id.*
[123] *Id.* at 333.
[124] *Id.* at 332.
[125] *Id.*
[126] *Id.* at 333.
[127] *Id.*
[128] Glen Weldon, *New Year, New Changes; Also, FLEX MENTALLO! HERO OF THE BEACH!*, Jan. 5, 2011, NPR.com, http://www.npr.org/sections/monkeysee/2011/01/05/132672533/new-year-new-changes-also-flex-mentallo-hero-of-the-beach (last visited January 25, 2017). *See also* Brian Cronin, *Comic Book Legends Revealed #284*, Oct. 29, 2010, http://goodcomics.comicbookresources.com/2010/10/29/comic-book-legends-revealed-284/ (last visited January 25, 2017).

[129] Chris Arrant, *Doom Patrol Leads New DC Imprint by Gerard Way*, April 07, 2016, Newsarama.com, http://www.newsarama.com/28744-doom-patrol-leads-new-dc-imprint-by-gerard-way.html (last visited January 25, 2017).
[130] *See Doom Patrol No. 3* (2016).
[131] Charles Atlas, Ltd., 112 F.Supp.2d at 339.
[132] *Id.* at 340.
[133] *Id.*
[134] *Id.* at 334.
[135] Chris Arrant, *Doom Patrol Leads New DC Imprint by Gerard Way*, April 07, 2016, Newsarama.com, http://www.newsarama.com/28744-doom-patrol-leads-new-dc-imprint-by-gerard-way.html (last visited January 25, 2017).
[136] Detective Comics, Inc. v. Bruns Publications, Inc., 111 F.2d 432, 433 (2nd Cir. 1940).
[137] *Id.*
[138] *Id.*

[139] *Id.* at 433-34.
[140] Warner Bros., Inc. v. American Broadcasting Companies, Inc., 720 F.2d 231, 238 (2nd Cir. 1983).
[141] *Id.* at 236.
[142] *Id.*
[143] *Id.* at 237.
[144] *Id.*
[145] *Id.* at 243.
[146] 17 U.S.C. §106(1).
[147] 17 U.S.C. §106(2).
[148] 17 §107.
[149] Campbell v. Acuff-Rose Music, Inc., 510 U.S. 569, 579 (1994).
[150] *Id.* at 580.
[151] *Id.* at 581.
[152] Comedy III Prods. V. Gary Saderup, Inc., 106 Cal.Rptr.2d 126, 131 (Cal. 2001).
[153] *Id.*
[154] *Id.*
[155] *Id.* at 130.
[156] *Id.* at 127.
[157] *Id.* at 136.
[158] ETW Corp. v. Jireh Pub., Inc., 332 F.3d 915, 918 (6th Cir. 2003).
[159] *Id.* at 919.
[160] *Id.*
[161] *Id.* at 920-21.
[162] *Id.* at 937.
[163] *Id.* at 938.
[164] Univ. of Ala. Bd. of Trs. V. New Life Art, Inc. 683 F.3d 1266, 1270 (11th Cir. 2012).
[165] *Id.*
[166] *Id.*
[167] *Id.* at 1275.
[168] *Id.* at 1278-79.
[169] Warner Bros. Ent., Inc. v. Rdr Books, 575 F.Supp.2d 513, 520 (S.D.N.Y. 2008).
[170] *Id.* at 520.
[171] *Id.* at 521.
[172] *Id.* at 521-22.
[173] *Id.* at 524.
[174] *Id.* at 538.
[175] *Id.* at 551.
[176] *Id.*
[177] *Id.* at 539.
[178] *Id.* at 551.
[179] *Id.* at 554.

[180] Steve VanderArk, *Publication of the New Lexicon Book*, Dec. 5, 2008, https://www.hp-lexicon.org/2008/12/05/publication-of-the-new-lexicon-book/ (last visited January 25, 2017).
[181] Walker v. DC Comics, No. 02-3058, at 2 (3rd Cir. Filed June 18, 2003).
[182] *Id.*
[183] *Id.*
[184] *Id.* at 3.
[185] *Id.*
[186] *Id.* at 3-4.
[187] *Id.* at 4.
[188] *Id.*, quoting Dam Things from Denmark v. Russ Berrie & Co., Inc., 290 F.3d 548, 563 (3rd Cir. 2002).
[189] Siegel v. Time Warner, Inc., 496 F.Supp.2d 1111, 1113 (C.D. Cal. 2007).
[190] Id.
[191] Id. at 1114.
[192] Id.
[193] Id.
[194] Id.
[195] Id.
[196] Id.
[197] Siegel v. National Periodical Publications, Inc., 508 F.2d 909, 911 (2nd Cir. 1974).
[198] Siegel v. Time Warner, Inc., 496 F.Supp.2d 1111, 1114 (C.D. Cal. 2007).
[199] Id. at 1114-15.
[200] Id.
[201] Id. at 1115.
[202] Id.
[203] Id.
[204] Id.
[205] Id. at 1115-16.
[206] Id. at 1116.
[207] Id.
[208] Id.
[209] Id. at 1118.
[210] Id.
[211] Id.
[212] *See* Copyright Act of 1909, § 23, http://www.copyright.gov/history/1909act.pdf (last visited January 25, 2017).
[213] Id.
[214] Id.
[215] Siegel v. Time Warner, Inc., 496 F.Supp.2d 1111, 1119 (C.D. Cal. 2007).
[216] Siegel v. National Periodical Publications, Inc., 364 F.Supp. 1032, 1035 (S.D.N.Y. 1973).
[217] Id.
[218] Id. at 1036.

[219] Id. at 1037
[220] Id. at 1036.
[221] Siegel v. National Periodical Publicatoins, Inc., 508 F.2d 909, 912-14 (2nd Cir. 1974).
[222] Id. at 914.
[223] Mary Breasted, *Superman's Creators, Nearly Destitute, Invoke His Spirit*, N.Y. TIMES, Nov. 22, 1975, http://www.nytimes.com/1975/11/22/archives/supermans-creators-nearly-destitute-invoke-his-spirit.html?_r=0 (last visited January 25, 2017).
[224] Id.
[225] Id.
[226] Siegel v. Warner Bros. Entertainment, Inc., 542 F.Supp.2d 1098, 1113 (C.D. Cal. 2008).
[227] Id.
[228] Id.
[229] DC Comics v. Pacific Pictures Corp., No. 10-3633, at 2 (C.D. Cal. Oct. 17, 2012); Bruce Lambert, *Joseph Shuster, Cartoonist, Dies; Co-Creator of Superman Was 78*, N.Y. Times, Aug. 3, 1992, http://www.nytimes.com/1992/08/03/arts/joseph-shuster-cartoonist-dies-co-creator-of-superman-was-78.html (last visited January 25, 2017).
[230] Bruce Lambert, *Joseph Shuster, Cartoonist, Dies; Co-Creator of Superman Was 78*, N.Y. Times, Aug. 3, 1992, http://www.nytimes.com/1992/08/03/arts/joseph-shuster-cartoonist-dies-co-creator-of-superman-was-78.html (last visited January 25, 2017).
[231] Siegel, 542 F. Supp.2d at 1113.
[232] Id.
[233] Id.
[234] Id.
[235] DC Comics v. Pacific Pictures Corp., No. 10-3633, at 3.
[236] Id. at 4.
[237] Id. at 5.
[238] Id. at 3.
[239] *See* 17 U.S.C. §304(c).
[240] *See* 17 U.S.C. §304(d).
[241] Id.
[242] Siegel v. Warner Bros. Ent., Inc., 542 F.Supp.2d 1098, 1114 (C.D. Cal. 2008).
[243] Id.
[244] Id.
[245] Id.
[246] Id. at 1115.
[247] Larson v. Warner Bros. Ent., Inc., No. 2:04-cv-08776, at page 9, (C.D. Cal. April 18, 2013).
[248] Siegel, 542 F. Supp.2d at 1114.
[249] Id.
[250] Id.

[251] Id. at 1115-16.
[252] Id. at 1116.
[253] Id.
[254] Id.
[255] Id. at 1145.
[256] Siegel v. Warner Bros. Ent., Inc., 658 F.Supp.2d 1036, 1095 (C.D. Cal. 2009); 504 F. App'x 586.
[257] Larson v. Warner Bros. Ent., Inc., No. 11-55863, at page 3, (9th Cir. Jan. 10, 2013).
[258] Id. at 4-5.
[259] Larson v. Warner Bros. Ent., Inc., No. 2:04-cv-08776, at page 2, (C.D. Cal. April 18, 2013).
[260] Larson v. Warner Bros. Ent., Inc., No. 13-56243 at page 6 (9th Cir. Feb. 10, 2016).
[261] Id.
[262] DC Comics v. Pacific Pictures Corp., No. 10-3633, at 13 (C.D. Cal. Oct. 17, 2012).

www.ingramcontent.com/pod-product-compliance
Lightning Source LLC
Chambersburg PA
CBHW060421190526
45169CB00002B/997